CAVEMAN GUMBO

COLLECTED WIT AND WISDOM

WILL BRADY

DAVE CROSS

BEACHTOWN PUBLICATIONS
LAGUNA BEACH CALIFORNIA

PREFACE

"An apple a day keeps the doctor away." "What goes around, comes around." "No pain, no gain." Phrases like these stick, become clichés. Aphorisms, jokes, quotations, anecdotes, ancient observations, song lyrics, T-shirts, greeting cards, movie dialog, bumper stickers, bubble-gum wrapper horoscopes, something scratched on a restroom stall--"the jazz riffs of thinking," unexpected turns, humorous resolutions, the familiar made fresh. They come from philosophers, comedians, politicians, artists, teachers, friends, and many unknown sources. Bits of wit and wisdom parading through our consciousness.

The inspiration for this compilation comes from Willy, who organized and generated the first volume and then invited Dave to collaborate. It has been a natural partnership; the two have been good buddies for 45+ years, played hundreds of gigs together--musicians, teachers, husbands, dads, now geezers--a lot in common (a joke over a cold pitcher has always sounded good).

This collection is meant to be read randomly; we hope the reader takes as much pleasure in exploring this volume as we did in compiling it. Apologies for any omissions of the reader's own catalog of favorite wit and wisdom. We leave a few blank pages at the end of the book for your profound, timely, or humorous additions.

CONTENTS

ANIMALS

The great pleasure of a dog is that you may make a fool of yourself with him and not only will he not scold you, but he will make a fool of himself, too. (Samuel Butler)

It is of interest to note that while some dolphins are reported to have learned English---up to fifty words used in correct context---no human being has been reported to have learned dolphinese. (Carl Sagan)

Dogs laugh, but they laugh with their tails. (Max Eastman)

In the "Dennis the Menace" cartoon series, by Hank Ketcham, Dennis' cat is named "Hot Dog."

If toast always lands butter-side down and cats always land on their feet, what happens when you strap toast to the back of a cat and drop it? (Steven Wright)

To err is human, to forgive, canine.

I once had a sparrow alight upon my shoulder for a moment while I was hoeing in a village garden, and I felt that I was more distinguished by that circumstance than I should have been by any epaulet I could have worn. (Henry David Thoreau)

Poodles aren't as absorbent as they look.

Man is the only kind of varmint that sets his own trap, baits it, then steps in it. (John Steinbeck)

Nothing in the world is friendlier than a wet dog.

I've just bought a Border collie. The one I already had wasn't bored enough.

Man is rated the highest animal, at least among all animals that returned the questionnaire. (Robert Bralt)

If there are no dogs in Heaven, then when I die I want to go where they went. (Will Rogers)

When a cow laughs, does milk come out her nose?

Adam blamed Eve. Eve blamed the snake. The snake didn't have a leg to stand on.

A dog wags its tail with its heart. (Martin Buxbaum)

You can always tell about somebody by the way they put their hands on an animal. (Betty White)

We can judge the heart of a man by his treatment of animals. (Immanuel Kant)

Sign in a veterinarian's office: The doctor is in. Sit. Stay. (Gale Shipley)

My favorite animal is steak. (Fran Lebowitz)

Dogs lead a nice life. You never see a dog with a wristwatch. (George Carlin)

I gave my cat a bath the other day; they love it. He enjoyed it; it was fun for me. The fur would stick to my tongue, but other than that... (Steve Martin)

I have cats because they have no artificially imposed, culturally prescribed sense of decorum. They live in the moment. If I had an aneurysm in the brain and dropped dead, I love knowing that as the paramedics carry me out, my cats are going to be swatting at that little toe tag. (Paul Provenza)

It is just like man's vanity and impertinence to call an animal dumb because it is dumb to his dull perceptions. (Mark Twain)

Butterflies taste with their feet.

There is no snooze button on a cat who wants his breakfast. (Funny Times)

A bird does not sing because it has an answer. It sings because it has a song. (Chinese Proverb)

There is no psychiatrist in the world like a puppy licking your face. (Bern Williams)

It's practically impossible to look at a penguin and feel angry.

Aerodynamically the bumblebee shouldn't be able to fly, but the bumblebee doesn't know that, so it goes on flying anyway. (Mary Kay Ash)

What do you get when you cross a pit bull with a collie?...A dog that rips your leg off, then goes for help.

If cats could talk, they wouldn't. (Nan Porter)

DOG DIARY
8:00 am - Dog food! My favorite thing!
9:30 am - A car ride! My favorite thing!
9:40 am - A walk in the park! My favorite thing!
10:30 am - Got rubbed and petted! My favorite thing!
12:00 pm - Lunch! My favorite thing!
1:00 pm - Played in the yard! My favorite thing!
3:00 pm - Wagged my tail! My favorite thing!
5:00 pm - Milk bones! My favorite thing!
7:00 pm - Got to play ball! My favorite thing!

8:00 pm - Wow! Watched TV with the people! My favorite thing!
11:00 pm - Sleeping on the bed! My favorite thing!

One thing my dogs and I have in common is that we never want me to go to work.

Cats are intended to teach us that not everything in nature has a purpose. (Garrison Keillor)

Even snakes are afraid of snakes. (Steven Wright)

Mama bear to sleepless papa bear: "How many times have I told you, no coffee after September!"

Man is a rational animal who always loses his temper when called upon to act in accordance with the dictates of reason. (Orson Welles)

A racehorse is an animal that can take several thousand people for a ride at the same time.

Dogs have owners. Cats have staff.

Two female ostriches were walking down the beach when they noticed two male ostriches running towards them.
One girl says to the other, "Oh-oh, here come those rowdy boys...we better hide," and they stuck their heads into the sand.
The two male ostriches run up, stop and look around. One says to the other, "Hey...where'd they go?"

A cat can purr its way out of anything. (Donna McCrohan)

Why do cows have hooves?...Because they lactose. (AARP Magazine)

Whose cow speaks Russian?...Ma's cow.

You can say any foolish thing to a dog, and the dog will give you a look that says, "My God, you're right! I never would have thought of that!" (Dave Barry)

Posted on a bulletin board: Mixed-breed puppies, $500 each. Ask about special $500 rebate.

If you think your dog can't count, try putting three dog treats in your pocket and then give him two of them.

Thousands of years ago cats were worshipped as gods. Cats have never forgotten this.

The dog is a gentleman; I hope to go to his heaven, not Man's. (Mark Twain)

You cannot look at a sleeping cat and feel tense. (Jane Pauley)

What do you get when you cross an elephant with a rhino?...Elephino?! (Bill Webb)

FIRST DOG: I can't figure it out. I'm in perfect physical shape, but I'm constantly anxious.
SECOND DOG: Why don't you go to a psychiatrist?
FIRST DOG: How can I? I'm not allowed on the couch.

Outside of a dog, a book is a man's best friend. Inside a dog it is too dark to read. (Groucho Marx)

Dogs come when they're called; Cats take a message and get back to you.

When a dog runs at you, whistle for him. (Henry David Thoreau)

BABY SNAKE: Mommy, are we poisonous?
MAMA SNAKE: Why do you ask?
BABY SNAKE: I just bit my tongue.

It's all about perspective. The sinking of the Titanic was a miracle to the lobsters in the ship's kitchen.

Horse sense is the thing a horse has which keeps it from betting on people. (W. C. Fields)

The problem with cats is they get the exact same look whether they see a moth or an axe murderer. (Paula Poundstone)

Don't accept your dog's admiration as conclusive evidence that you are wonderful. (Ann Landers)

This weekend I'm attending an animal rights barbecue.

Two penguins are standing on an iceberg. One penguin says to the other, "You look like you're wearing a tuxedo." The other penguin replies, "Who says I'm not?"

It is not the strongest of the species that survive, nor the most intelligent, but the one most responsive to change. (Charles Darwin)

Man is the only animal that blushes. Or needs to. (Mark Twain)

I like pigs. Dogs look up to us. Cats look down on us. Pigs treat us as equals. (Winston Churchill)

ARTS

I love Beethoven, especially the poems. (Ringo Starr)

Music is not illusion, but revelation rather. Its triumphant power resides in the fact that it reveals to us beauties we find nowhere else. (Peter Ilyich Tchaikovsky)

He has Van Gogh's ear for music. (Billy Wilder)

I used to be in a band called 'Missing Dog'. You probably saw our posters.

Love of beauty is taste. The creation of beauty is art. (Ralph Waldo Emerson)

Life doesn't imitate art, it imitates bad television. (Woody Allen)

Interviewer: How much rewriting do you do?
Hemingway: It depends. I rewrote the ending of *A Farewell to Arms*, the last page of it, thirty-nine times before I was satisfied.
Interviewer: Was there some technical problem there? What was it that had you stumped?
Hemingway: Getting the words right. (Paris Review)

I didn't like the play. But I saw it under unfavorable circumstances...the curtains were up. (Groucho Marx)

Find me playing 'til sunrise for fifty cents and a sandwich. (Muddy Waters)

He was a fiddler, and consequently a rogue. (Jonathan Swift)

Every artist was first an amateur. (Ralph Waldo Emerson)

7

Go to High School. Write down everything. (Taylor Swift on songwriting)

Some people have a way with words, others not have way.

He who works with his hands is a laborer. He who works with his hands and his head is a craftsman. He who works with his hands, his head and his heart is an artist. (Saint Francis of Assisi)

Anything played wrong twice in a row is the beginning of an arrangement. (Frank Zappa)

Fiction reveals truth that reality obscures. (Ralph Waldo Emerson)

Music attracts the angels in the universe. (Bob Dylan)

Books, the children of the brain. (Jonathan Swift)

Why couldn't I
Have known before so long,
Nothing for the singer,
Everything for the song. (written on the Green Room wall, the Troubadour, 1964)

You think your pains and heartbreaks are unprecedented in the history of the world, but then you read. It was books that taught me that things that tormented me were the very things that connected me with all the people who were alive, or who have ever been alive. (James Baldwin)

Paris is for Louvres. (T-shirt)

A musician wins $75,000 in the lottery.
TV interviewer: May I ask you what you do for a living?
Musician: I'm a full-time musician.
TV interviewer: $75,000...that's a lot of money. If you don't mind me asking, what do you expect to do with it?
Musician: I guess I'll just keep working until it's gone.

It is better to have done something than to have been someone. (Claude Monet)

I can play piano with my eyes closed. It sounds really awful though.

Beauty in things exists in the mind that contemplates them. (David Hume)

When you hit a wrong note, it's the next note that makes it good or bad. (Miles Davis)

I'm not a great musician, I'm a grateful musician. I rose to the top of the bottom of the music business. (Dave Cross)

The historian will tell you what happened. The novelist will tell you what it felt like. (E. L. Doctorow)

Nothing cooks itself. (drummer Bill Meeker)

After watching a performance of his play *Peter Pan* with his five-year-old godson, J. M. Barrie asked the boy what he had liked best. "What I think I liked best," the boy replied, "was tearing up the program and dropping the bits on people's heads." (Lapham's Quarterly)

Fiction is obliged to stick to possibilities. Truth isn't. (Mark Twain)

Since I didn't have any kind of formal training, it didn't make any difference to me if I was listening to Lightnin' Slim, or a vocal group called the Jewels...or Webern, or Varese, or Stravinsky. To me it was all good music. (Frank Zappa)

My mother said that songs came through God, and I'd like to believe that might be true. (Johnny Cash)

An essential thing was mystery. That was what dreams and truly great works of art had in common. Mystery. (Herman Hesse, "Narcissus and Goldman," 1930)

A movie is life with the dull parts cut out. (Alfred Hitchcock)

Mozart is sunshine. (Antonin Dvorak)

Boy (to mom): When I grow up I want to be a musician! Mom: I'm sorry, Honey, you can't do both.

The man who has no imagination has no wings. (Mohammad Ali)

It is the function of art to renew our perception. What we are familiar with we cease to see. The writer shakes up the familiar scene, and, as if by magic, we see a new meaning in it. (Anais Nin)

I tried to write a drinking song, but I couldn't make it past the first few bars.

I've always held the song in high regard because songs have got me through so many sinks of dishes and so many humiliating courting events. (Leonard Cohen)

An artist is someone who has learned to trust in himself. (Ludwig van Beethoven)

Art is either plagiarism or revolution. (Paul Gauguin)

It's taken me all my life to learn what not to play. (Dizzy Gillespie)

The most important thing I look for in a musician is whether he knows how to listen. (Duke Ellington)

Frustration is one of the greatest things in art; satisfaction is nothing. (Malcom McLaren)

Everything you can imagine is real. (Pablo Picasso)

You have to create the quiet to be able to listen to the very faint voice of your intuition. (Jon Favreau)

What's green and sings?...Elvis Parsley.

I have won several prizes as the world's slowest alto player, as well as a special award in 1961 for quietness. (Paul Desmond)

I think I had it in the back of my mind that I wanted to sound like a dry martini. (Paul Desmond)

I was unfashionable before anyone knew who I was. (Paul Desmond)

I tried practicing for a few weeks and ended up playing too fast. (Paul Desmond)

My life is music, and in some vague, mysterious and subconscious way, I have always been driven by a taut inner spring which has propelled me to almost compulsively reach for perfection in music, often—in fact, mostly—at the expense of everything else in my life. (Stan Getz)

When asked, "How do you write?" I invariably answer, "One word at a time," and the answer is invariably dismissed. But that is all it is. It sounds too simple to be true, but consider the Great Wall of China, if you will: One stone at a time, man. One stone at a time. But I've read you can see that mother from space without a telescope. (Steven King)

I was trying to play guitar like John Coltrane played the sax. Of course, nobody understood it, especially me. (James Gurley-Big Brother & the Holding Company, 1968)

In fifteen seconds the difference between composition and improvisation is that in composition you have all the time you want to decide what to say in fifteen seconds, while in improvisation you have fifteen seconds. (Steve Lacy)

Guitar players read by ear. (Ron Eschete)

It Don't Mean a Thing, If It Ain't Got That Swing. (Duke Ellington-1943)

Music is the most physically inspiring of all the arts. (Frank Zappa)

Playing 'bop' is like playing Scrabble with all the vowels missing. (Duke Ellington)

I like beautiful melodies telling you terrible things. (Tom Waits)

Hell, there ain't no notes on the banjo. You just play it!

Art is by nature optimistic. Art is optimistic because it is alive. (Patti Smith)

I have had a very thin time of it these days. My money ran out on Thursday, and I have lived for four days on twenty-three cups of coffee. (Vincent van Gogh)

Practice makes perfect, and nobody's perfect, so why practice? (David Dean)

The composer Stravinsky had written a new piece with a difficult violin passage. After it had been in rehearsal for several weeks, the solo violinist came to Stravinsky and said he was sorry, he had tried his best, the passage was too difficult, no violinist could play it. Stravinsky said, "I understand that. What I am after is the sound of someone trying to play it." (Thomas Powers)

After silence, that which comes nearest to expressing the inexpressible is music. (Aldous Huxley)

My neighbor banged on my front door at 2:30 this morning. Thank God I was still up playing the drums.

Two grooves in country music: 'dook-a-chucka' and 'clip-clop.' (drummer Bill Meeker)

A22DNCR (License Plate)

Write about winter in the summer. Describe Norway as Ibsen did, from a desk in Paris. Willa Cather wrote her prairie novels in New York City. Mark Twain wrote *Huckleberry Finn* in Hartford. Recently, scholars learned that Walt Whitman rarely left his room. (Annie Dillard)

The worst thing that can happen to a writer is to become a writer. (Mary McCarthy)

He who sings scares away his woes. (Spanish Proverb)

When the mbira is played it brings the two worlds together, the world of our ancestors and the world of today. (Ephat Mujuru, mbira [thumb piano] player from Zimbabwe)

I don't know anything about music. In my line you don't have to. (Elvis Presley)

What do Fellini's films have to do with naturalism? He works with the inaccuracies of memory. It's the opposite direction from naturalism: elevating things to mythical, archetypal status. Make them more dreamlike. That's a feeling I like a lot. (Brian Eno)

First thoughts are the strongest. (Allen Ginsberg)

Art is the stored honey of the human soul, gathered on wings of misery and travail. (Theodore Dreiser)

What did Vincent say when his car was stolen?...Where did my Van Gogh?

Why should people go out and pay money to see bad films when they can stay home and see bad television for nothing? (Samuel Goldwyn)

My books are water; those of the great geniuses are wine. Everybody drinks water. (Mark Twain)

How is a drum solo like a sneeze?...You can tell it's coming, but you can't do anything about it.

A poet looks at the world as a man looks at a woman. (Wallace Stevens)

This urge to make everything profound. What nonsense! (Henry Miller)

I dream my painting, and then I paint my dream. (Vincent Van Gogh)

How many poets does it take to screw in a lightbulb? Two: One to curse the darkness, and one to light a candle.

I don't paint things. I only paint the difference between things. (Henry Matisse)

A classic is something that everybody wants to have read and nobody wants to read. (Mark Twain)

Making the simple complicated is commonplace; making the complicated simple, awesomely simple, that's creative. (Charles Mingus)

Information is not knowledge. Knowledge is not wisdom. Wisdom is not truth. Truth is not beauty. Beauty is not love. Love is not music. Music is the best. (Frank Zappa)

"I used to drive out to John's house," says Paul McCartney. "He lived out in the country, and I lived in London. I remember asking the chauffeur once if he was having a good week. He said, 'I'm very busy at the moment. I've been working eight days a week.' And I thought, 'Eight days a week! Now there's a title.'"

Charles Dickens walks into a bar and orders a martini. The bartender asks, "Olive or Twist?"

Give me a smart idiot over a stupid genius any day. (Samuel Goldwyn)

For a long time now I have tried simply to write the best I can. Sometimes I get lucky and write better than I can. (Ernest Hemingway)

I kept writing not because I felt I was so good, but because I thought they were so bad, including Shakespeare, all those. The stilted formalism, like chewing cardboard. (Charles Bukowski)

TRNTBLS (License plate)

I hate flowers. I paint them because they're cheaper than models and they don't move. (Georgia O'Keefe)

Tuba Player: Did you hear my last recital?
Friend: I hope so.

For a long time now I have tried simply to write the best I can. Sometimes I get lucky and write better than I can. (Ernest Hemingway)

A person from Boston took a Zen Buddhist monk to hear the Boston Symphony perform Beethoven's Fifth Symphony. His comment was, "Not enough silence."

Art should never try to be popular. The public should try to make itself artistic. (Oscar Wilde)

In the 1960s when the recording studio suddenly really took off as a tool, it was the kids from art school who knew how to use it, not the kids from music school. Music students were all stuck in the notion of music as performance, ephemeral. Whereas for art students, music as painting? They knew how to do that. (Brian Eno)

(On writing) There are days when the result is so bad that no fewer than five revisions are required. In contrast, when I'm greatly inspired, only four revisions are needed. (John Kenneth Galbraith)

Interviewer: Some people say they can't understand your writing even after they read it two or three times. What approach would you suggest for them?
William Faulkner: Read it four times.

To say that a work of art is good, but incomprehensible to the majority of men, is the same as saying of some kind of food that it is very good but that most people can't eat it. (Leo Tolstoy)

What is art but a way of seeing? (Saul Bellow)

It takes a very good drummer to be better than no drummer at all. (Chet Baker)

Nowhere is Hell so paved with good intentions as in Art. (Aldous Huxley)

Two girls are walking through the forest when they come upon a talking frog. "Kiss me and I will turn into a famous jazz musician," says the frog.
The first girl picks him up and puts him in her purse.
"How come you didn't kiss him?" says the other girl.
"He'll be worth a lot more as a talking frog," says the first.

Artistic growth is, more than it is anything else, a refining of the sense of truthfulness. The stupid believe that to be truthful is easy; only the artist, the great artist, knows how difficult it is. (Willa Cather)

If I miss one day of practice, I can tell. Two days: the critics can tell. Three days: the public can tell. (Yascha Heifitz)

Having your book turned into a movie is like seeing your oxen turned into bouillon cubes. (John le Carre)

Three chords and the truth---That's what a country song is. (Willie Nelson)

Too many pieces of music finish too long after the end. (Igor Stravinsky)
The secret to being funny is to say smart things stupidly. Or is it stupid things smartly? Whatever...It's not rocket surgery.

Did you hear about the tenor who was so arrogant that even the other tenors noticed?

George Bernard Shaw telegram to Winston Churchill: "Sending you two opening night tickets to my new play. Bring a friend if you have one." Winston Churchill to Shaw: "Unable to come on opening night. Will come 2nd night, if you have one."

Those who wish to sing always find a song. (Swedish Proverb)

If it sounds good, it *is* good. (Duke Ellington)

There are no wrong notes...only wrong resolutions. (Dizzy Gillespie)

Miles Davis (on how to begin a solo): "Think of a note...then don't play it."

When composer Igor Stravinsky was fifty-seven, he settled in the United States and a year later decided to apply for American citizenship. He made an appointment to see the appropriate official. At his first interview the official asked the famous composer his name. "Stra-vin-sky," he replied, speaking each syllable distinctly. "You could change it, you know," suggested the official. (Bartlett's Book of Anecdotes)

Where words fail, music speaks. (Hans Christian Anderson)

The music business is a cruel and shallow money trench, a long plastic highway where thieves and pimps run free, and good men die like dogs. There's also a negative side. (Hunter S. Thompson)

MUDEH2O (License plate)

How many producers does it take to screw in a lightbulb?...I don't know...what do you think?

The difference between fiction and reality? Fiction has to make sense. (Tom Clancy)

The great composer does not set to work because he is inspired, but becomes inspired because he is working. Beethoven, Wagner, Bach, and Mozart settled down day after day to the job in hand with as much regularity as an accountant settles down each day to his figures. They didn't waste time waiting for inspiration. (Ernest Newman)

How many surrealists does it take to change a lightbulb?...Two: One to hold the giraffe, and the other to fill the bathtub with brightly colored machine tools.

What's the difference between an accordion and an onion?...Nobody cries when you chop up an accordion.

All the sounds of the earth are like music. (Oscar Hammerstein)

There are no dull subjects, there are only dull writers. (H. L. Mencken)

I decided to start anew---to strip away what I had been taught, to accept as true my own thinking. This was one of the best times of my life. There was no one around to look at what I was doing, no one interested, no one to say anything about it one way or another. I was alone and singularly free, working into my own, unknown---no one to satisfy but myself. I began with charcoal and paper and decided not to use any color until it was impossible to do what I wanted to do in black and white. I believe it was June before I needed blue. (Georgia O'Keefe)

There's no money in poetry...but then there's no poetry in money, either. (Robert Graves)

Amatuers copy, pros steal

I knew a one-armed piano player once...It took him two minutes to play "The Minute Waltz."

What's the difference between a trumpet and a trombone?...You can make more belt-buckles out of a trombone.

I perhaps owe having become a painter to the flowers. (Claude Monet)

When I don't write, I feel my world shrinking. I feel I am in a prison. I feel I lose my fire and my color. It should be a necessity, as the sea needs to heave, and I call it breathing. (Anais Nin)

You want to make money in the music business?...sell band uniforms. (Andre Previn)

Art is a luxury for which the artist pays. (David Smith, sculptor)

Church for accordion players...Our Lady of Spain.

Television has raised writing to a new low. (Samuel Goldwyn)

You never have to change anything you got up in the middle of the night to write. (Saul Bellow)

After a concert, a fan rushed up to famed violinist Fritz Kreisler and gushed: "I'd give my life to play as beautifully as you do." Kreisler replied, "I did."

Things are beautiful if you love them. (Jean Anouilh)

Shelly Manne, famous jazz drummer, was once in a serious car accident. As he was being hurried to the ER on a gurney, the attendant asked, "Is there anything you can't take?" Shelley replied, "Country music."

Never judge a book by its movie. (J.W. Eagan)

It is difficult to produce a television documentary that is both incisive and probing when every 12 minutes one is interrupted by 12 dancing rabbits singing about toilet paper. (Rod Serling)

An intellectual snob is someone who can listen to the William Tell Overture and not think of The Lone Ranger. (Dan Rather)

I hate music, especially when it's played. (Jimmy Durante)

The chromatic scale is what you use to give the effect of drinking a quinine martini and having an enema simultaneously. (Philip Larkin)

Music is the language of the spirit. It opens the secret of life, bringing peace, abolishing strife. (Kahlil Gibran)

Classical music is the kind we keep thinking will turn into a tune. (Kin Hubbard)

Assassins! (Arturo Toscanini to his orchestra)

The chief objection to playing wind instruments is that it prolongs the life of the player. (George Bernard Shaw)

Harpists spend ninety percent of their lives tuning their harps and ten percent playing out of tune. (Igor Stravinsky)

You can't wait for inspiration. You must go after it with a club. (Jack London)

Wagner's music is better than it sounds. (Mark Twain)

Man is not on the earth solely for his own happiness. He is there to realize great things for humanity. (Vincent Van Gogh)

A story should have a beginning, a middle, and an end…but not necessarily in that order. (Jean Luc Goddard)

The amount of money one needs is terrifying. (Ludwig Van Beethoven)

You can't possibly hear the last movement of Beethoven's Seventh and go slow. (Oscar Levant, explaining his way out of a speeding ticket)

PATIENT: Doc, you've got to help me! Every time I drive down a country lane, I find myself singing 'Green Green

Grass Of Home.' Every time I see a cat I sing 'What's New Pussycat?' And last night I sang 'Delilah' in my sleep. I tell you, Doc, my wife was not at all amused.
DOCTOR: I wouldn't worry. It seems you have the early symptoms of Tom Jones syndrome.
PATIENT: I have never heard of that. Is it common?
DOCTOR: It's not unusual.

There are only two kinds of songs: the blues and zip-a-dee-doo-dah. (Townes Van Zandt)

Music is organized sound. (Edgard Varese)

The road to Hell is paved with adverbs. (Stephen King)

General Custer and an Indian scout are on top of a hill overlooking Little Big Horn, when they start to hear drums in the distance. General Custer says, "I don't like the sound of those drums." The Indian scout listens for a second and says, "That's not their regular drummer."

Dare to be stupid. (Weird Al Yankovic)

If you create from the heart, nearly everything works: if from the head, almost nothing. (Marc Chagall)

There are three rules for writing a novel. Unfortunately, no one knows what they are. (W. Somerset Maugham)

All the inspiration I ever needed was a phone call from a producer. (Cole Porter)

If Isaac Stern tries to play every piece ever composed for the violin, would he leave no tone un-Sterned?

He has never been known to use a word that might send a reader to the dictionary. (William Faulkner about Ernest Hemingway)

Thank you for sending me a copy of your book; I'll waste no time reading it. (Moses Hadas)

Opera is where a guy gets stabbed in the back, and instead of dying, he sings. (Robert Benchley)

Everything has beauty, but not everyone sees it. (Confucius)

Never look at the trombones, it only encourages them. (Richard Strauss)

Over the years I have discovered that ideas come through an intense desire for them; continually desiring, the mind becomes a watchtower on the lookout for incidents that may excite the imagination. (Charlie Chaplin)

A backward poet writes inverse.

We are not here to do what has already been done. (Robert Henri)

CLASSIFIED AD: "Apt. for rent: 3 br., deposit, lease. No poets."

Students in a Harvard English 101 class were asked to write a concise essay containing four elements: religion, royalty, sex and mystery. The only A+ in the class read: "My God," said the Queen, "I'm pregnant! I wonder who did it."

An idea comes as close to something for nothing as you can get. (Robert Frost)

1 million microphones=1 megaphone

The difference between the right word and almost the right word is like the difference between lightning and the lightning bug. (Mark Twain)

Learning music by reading about it is like making love by mail. (Luciano Pavarotti)

A writer is someone for whom writing is more difficult than it is for other people. (Thomas Mann)

Art is long and life is short. (Goethe)

Everybody has talent at 25. The difficult thing is to have it at 50. (Edgar Degas)

Art is making something out of nothing and selling it. (Frank Zappa)

The most important thing to succeed in show business is sincerity. And if you can fake that, you've got it made. (George Burns)

There is no surer way of evading the world than by Art, and no surer way of uniting with it than in Art. (Johann Wolfgang von Goethe)

How many altos does it take to screw in a lightbulb?...One to climb the ladder and the rest to complain about how high it is.

What's the difference between a soprano and a rottweiler?...Jewelry.

"My first real joke was in the fourth-grade talent show. My friend Joel wrapped himself up in bandages like a mummy and held a sign that read '400 B.C.' I said that was the license plate of the car that ran over him." (Jay Leno)

Inspiration only knocks. Some writers expect it to break down the door and pull them out of bed. (Leonard Bernstein)

Music is spiritual. The music business is not. (Van Morrison)

An artist is a man who carries his happiness within him. (Ludwig von Beethoven)

Books are the quietest and most constant of friends; they are the most accessible and wisest of counsellors, and the most patient of teachers. (Charles E. Eliot)

The eccentric American composer John Cage is responsible for composing the sheet music for his extremely quiet Opus "4 Minutes, 33 Seconds," which is exactly that much silence. The sheet music is blank and just tells you how long not to play.

Music gives a soul to the universe, wings to the mind, flight to the imagination, and life to everything. (Plato)

Last year I went fishing with Salvador Dali. He was using a dotted line. He caught every other fish. (Steven Wright)

I hold that a writer who does not passionately believe in the perfectibility of man has no dedication nor any membership in literature. (John Steinbeck)

I'll play it first and tell you what it is later. (Miles Davis)

Music is the shorthand of emotion. (Leo Tolstoy)

The most popular form of transportation in the music business is the bandwagon. (David Hopper)

Among the many forms in which human spirit has tried to express its innermost yearnings and perceptions, music is perhaps the most universal. It symbolizes the yearning for harmony, with oneself and others, with nature and the spiritual and the sacred within us and around us. There is something in music that transcends and unites. This is evident in the sacred music of every community...music that expresses the universal yearning that is shared by people all over the globe. (Dalai Lama)

Our good time is sitting in a coffee shop with a newspaper, writing a line on the back of a napkin. That is the most fun comedians ever have. (Jerry Seinfeld)

I'm writing a book. I've got the page numbers done. (Steven Wright)

Music is the meeting place of the tangible and the intangible. (Yehudi Mehnuin)

Sign on a music teacher's door: "Out Chopin, Bach in a minuet."

Audiences like their blues singers to be miserable. (Janis Joplin)

I did a theatrical performance about puns. It was a play on words. (M. D. Rosenberg)

It is said that no word in the English language rhymes with: month, orange, silver or purple. (See YouTube, Eminem Rhymes Orange)

I like talking about ideas. I find them terribly interesting. (Brian Eno)

Television is a medium. So called because it is neither rare nor well done. (Ernie Kovacs)

The hardest thing about writing is writing. (Nora Ephron)

How do you make a guitar player stop playing?...put some music in front of him. How do you make a violin player stop playing?...take the music away.

Les Paul, the great guitarist, was asked in an interview with Pat Martino (also a great guitarist): Do you have any guidelines for guitar players? He replied, "Can your Mom recognize your playing over the radio?"

To play a wrong note is insignificant; to play without passion is inexcusable. (Beethoven)

Genius is to believe your own thought; to believe that what is true for you in your private heart is true for all men. (Ralph Waldo Emerson)

Painting is another way of keeping a diary. (Pablo Picasso)

You can't use up creativity. The more you use, the more you have. (Maya Angelou)

Metaphors be with you (Bumper Sticker)

ATTITUDE

Ever notice that "what the hell" is always the right decision? (Marilyn Monroe)

Always be ready to speak your mind, and a base man will avoid you. (William Blake)

Once you've been really 'bad' in a movie, there's a certain kind of fearlessness you develop. (Jack Nicholson)

A clear conscience is usually the sign of a bad memory. (Stephen Wright)

Always do sober what you said you`d do drunk. That will teach you to keep your mouth shut. (Ernest Hemingway)

Remember me? I'm the one who's not you.

Ain't nobody's business if I bark like a dog. (Muddy Waters)

I can relax with bums because I am a bum. I don't like laws, morals, religions, rules. I don't like to be shaped by society. (Charles Bukowski)

It's kinda fun to hold the door open for people who are far away so they have to run a little! (Aaron Caro's Ruminations.com)

A professional is someone who can do his best work when he doesn't feel like it. (Alistair Cooke)

Act boldly and unseen forces will come to your aid. (Dorothea Brande)

People come up to me and say, "What's wrong?" Nothing. "Well, it takes more energy to frown than it does to smile." Yeah, well, it takes more energy to point that out than it does to leave me alone. (Bill Hicks)

RBRCHKN (License plate)

You can only be young once. But you can always be immature. (Dave Barry)

My doctors told me I would never walk again. My mother told me I would. I believed my mother. (Wilma Randolph, Olympic gold medalist)

All who wander are not lost. (Bumper Sticker)

Experience is not what happens to you. It's what you do with what happens to you. (Aldous Huxley)

Every saint has a past; every criminal has a future. (Oscar Wilde)

I'm not lost...I'm exploring (Bumper sticker)

Curious people are interesting people; I wonder why that is. (Bill Maher)

It's just a job. Grass grows, birds fly, waves pound the sand. I beat people up. (Muhammad Ali)

Bring the pure wine of love and freedom.
But Sir, a tornado is coming.
More wine, we will teach this storm
A thing or two about whirling. (Rumi)

If the fool would persist in his folly he would become wise. (William Blake)

When the stomach is full, it is easy to talk of fasting. (St. Jerome)

Wise men don't need advice; fools don't take it. (Benjamin Franklin)

Life does not cease to be funny when people die any more than it ceases to be serious when people laugh. (George Bernard Shaw)

Mouth shut, eyes open.

Always get eight hours of beauty sleep...nine if you're ugly. (Betty White)

Passionate hatred can give meaning and purpose to an empty life. (Eric Hoffer)

Whatever women do they must do twice as well as men to be thought half as good. Luckily this is not difficult. (Charlotte Whitton)

The human race has one really effective weapon, and that is laughter. (Mark Twain)

I realize that humor isn't for everyone. It's only for people who want to have fun, enjoy life, and feel alive. (Anne Wilson Scheal)

I am free of all prejudices. I hate everyone equally. (W. C. Fields)

Warming up fish in the microwave at work is the office equivalent of terrorism. (Aaron Karo's Ruminations.com)

Stupid people never forgive nor forget, the naive forgive and forget, the wise forgive but never forget. (Francois de La Rochefoucauld)

Answering machine message: "I am not available right now, but thank you for caring enough to call. I am making some changes in my life. Please leave a message after the beep. If I do not return your call, you are one of the changes."

I'm not going to be the person I am expected to be anymore. (Blue de Chanel)

God offers to every mind its choices between truth and repose. Take whichever you please; you can never have both. (Ralph Waldo Emerson)

We don't need to increase our goods nearly as much as we need to scale down our wants. Not wanting something is as good as possessing it. (Donald Horban)

He who justifies himself does not convince. (Lao Tzu)

Wanna go deaf for a few minutes? Bring a metal bolt to an amusement park. Get on the roller coaster with a person who looks terrified. When the ride starts, hold up the bolt and say, "Wait...where did this come from?" (Aaron Caro's Ruminations.com)

I got food poisoning today. I don't know when I'll use it. (Steven Wright)

Those who danced were thought to be quite insane by those who could not hear the music. (Angela Monet)

Before you criticize someone, walk a mile in their shoes. That way, when you criticize them, you're a mile away and you have their shoes.

You create your opportunities by asking for them. (Patty Hansen)

Therefore do not be anxious about tomorrow, for tomorrow will be anxious for itself. Sufficient unto the day is its own troubles. (Jesus, Matthew 6:34)

I used to pose in front of the mirror at home. I was hopeful. The only thing I was lacking was a bit of bread to buy an instrument. But I got the moves off first, and I got the guitar later. (Keith Richards)

Sometimes when I vacuum, I like to tease everyone else in the house by turning off the vacuum every once in a while for just enough time for them to think "Finally, he's done," then I turn it back on. (Aaron Karo-Ruminations.com)

He opens himself to all influences---everything nourishes him. Everything is gravy to him, including what he does not understand---particularly what he does not understand. (Henry Miller)

Never moon a werewolf.

Great spirits have always encountered violent opposition from mediocre minds. (Albert Einstein)

I'm not fat, I'm just easy to see.

Moderation is a fatal thing. Nothing succeeds like excess. (Oscar Wilde)

I couldn't wait for success…so I went ahead without it. (Jonathan Winters)

NAKMOUT (License plate)

A problem is a chance for you to do your best. (Duke Ellington)

You will do foolish things, but do them with enthusiasm. (Colette)

If you're going to do something tonight that you'll be sorry for tomorrow morning, sleep late. (Henny Youngman)

To have more, desire less.

Dip him in the river who loves water. (William Blake)

People who know little are usually great talkers, while men who know much say little. (Jean Jacques Rousseau)

People often say that this or that person has not yet found himself. But the self is not something that one finds. It is something one creates. (Thomas Szasz)

Being yourself is not remaining what you were, or being satisfied with what you are. It is the point of departure. (Sydney J. Harris)

Promises are either broken or kept.

To be wronged is nothing unless you continue to remember it. (Confucius)

Nothing ventured, nothing gained. Or as my friend, Dave Cross, puts it, "the fish don't jump in the boat."

A change is as good as a rest.

Seize the moment. Remember all those women on the Titanic who waved off the dessert cart. (Erma Bombeck)

You never get a second chance to make a first impression.

The fear of being laughed at makes cowards of us all. (Mignon McLaughlin)

A gentleman is someone who knows how to play the banjo and doesn't. (Mark Twain)

A wise man sometimes changes his mind, a fool never.

He who hesitates is lost; postponement is the father of failure. (ancient proverb)

Labor to keep alive in your breast that little spark of celestial fire called conscience. (George Washington)

To dare is to lose one's footing momentarily. Not to dare is to lose oneself. (Soren Kierkegaard)

I know a man who gave up smoking, drinking, sex, and rich food. He was healthy right up to the day he killed himself. (Johnny Carson)

Life has no remote. Get up and change it yourself.

Laughter and tears are both responses to frustration and exhaustion. I myself prefer to laugh, since there is less cleaning to do afterward. (Kurt Vonnegut)

If you could kick the person in the pants who is responsible for most of your troubles, you wouldn't sit for a month. (Theodore Roosevelt)

I've just written 'You have no new messages' on a piece of paper, put it in a bottle and thrown it far out to sea.

Bunny Berrigan was the nicest and sweetest bandleader of the swing era, and he had a sweet trumpet, too. He was also a terminal drunk who was dead by age 34. One time he was so drunk he couldn't stand up without leaning on the wall, but when it came time for his solo, he stepped up and knocked everybody's socks off. Afterward a girl asked him right out, "How can you be so drunk and still play so well?" He replied, "I practice drunk." (Dion Wright)

Wise men talk because they have something to say; fools, because they have to say something. (Plato)

I want to follow a random family around Disneyland for a day and just be in the background of all of their photos. (Aaron Karo-Ruminations.com)

Fight Apathy. Or Don't. (Graffiti)

BENT CLICHES

I think, therefore I am...thinking. (Dave Cross)

There must be a harder way to do this.

Oh, well, half of one, six dozen of the other. (Joe Garagiola)

Into each rain some life must fall. (Dave Cross)

You heard one cliché, you've heard them all. (Tom Tears)

Do onto others, then split. (Long Gone Miles)

Don't count your chickens with a hatchet. (Will Brady)

The lion and the calf shall lie down together but the calf won't get much sleep. (Woody Allen)

If you tell a joke in the forest, but nobody laughs, was it a joke? (Steven Wright)

You buttered your bread, now lie in it! (Janet Culp)

If the shoe fits, get another one just like it. (George Carlin)

I'll jump off that bridge when I come to it. (Adlai Stevenson)

Two wrongs don't make a right, but three rights make a left. (Paul Wagner)

It's onward and sideways. (Gail Chasin)

You have to learn to take the bad with the worse. (Dizzy Dean)

If I've told you once, I've told you a million times...Don't exaggerate. (David Banes)

Time is a great teacher, but unfortunately it kills all its pupils. (Hector Berlioz)

Absence makes the heart grow fungus.

I doubt, therefore I might be.

If at first you don't succeed, skydiving is not for you.

It is easier for a camel to pass through the eye of a needle if it's been though a blender first. (Les Barker)

If you've seen one shopping center, you've seen a mall.

A fool and his money are soon partying. (Will Brady)

There comes a time in every man's life, and I've had plenty of them. (Casey Stengel)

It's better to have loved and lost than never to have lost at all.

Where's there's smoke there's toast.

It's always darkest right before you stub your toe.

Caught between a rock and a hard-boiled egg.

The course of true love gathers no moss.

Nostalgia isn't what it used to be.

Someone sent me a postcard picture of the earth. On the back it said, "Wish you were here." (Steven Wright)

A day without sunshine is, like, night.

It's like the blond leading the blond.

If you can keep your head while all about you are losing theirs, you'll probably be the tallest guy in the room.

If at first you don't succeed, redefine success.

Quilters never weave, and weavers never quilt. (Sheldon Abbott)

Luck conquers all. (Will Brady)

ENVIRONMENT

The use of solar energy has not been opened up because the oil industry does not own the sun. (Ralph Nader)

Please save the earth. It's the only planet with chocolate. (Seen on a T-shirt)

Use it up, wear it out, make do, or do without. (Puritan saying)

Underground nuclear testing, defoliation of the rain forests, toxic waste...Let's put it this way: if the world were a big apartment, we wouldn't get our deposit back. (John Ross)

We could have saved the Earth but we were too damned cheap. (Kurt Vonnegut)

Never miss an opportunity of seeing anything beautiful, for beauty is God's handwriting. (Ralph Waldo Emerson)

It is not necessary to change. Survival is not mandatory. (W. Edwards Deming)

He who plants trees loves others besides himself. (English Proverb)

If you stand by the sea, it sounds like putting a shell to your ear.

It is horrifying that we have to fight our government to save the environment. (Ansel Adams)

I think the world will be saved by millions of small things. (Pete Seeger)

There is no alternative to water. (Bumper sticker)

Sign on a cabin wall: If there is something you need that you don't see, please let me know, and I'll show you how to do without it. (Richard Herman-Sun magazine)

When man invented the bicycle, he reached the peak of his attainments. Here was a machine of precision and balance for the convenience of man. And (unlike subsequent inventions for man's convenience) the more he used it, the fitter his body became. Here, for once, was a product of man's brain that was entirely beneficial to those who used it, and of no harm or irritation to others. Progress should have stopped when man invented the bicycle. (Elizabeth West)

Sponges grow in the ocean. This just kills me. I wonder how much deeper the ocean would be if that did not happen. (Steven Wright)

Every time I'm in the woods, I feel like I'm in church. (Pete Seeger)

Increasingly, the world around us looks as if we hated it. (Alan Watts)

Adopt the pace of nature: her secret is patience. (Ralph Waldo Emerson)

I'm optimistic about the future, but not about the future of this civilization. I'm optimistic about the civilization that will replace it. (James Baldwin)

Climb the mountains and get their good tidings. Nature's peace will flow into you as sunshine flows into trees. The winds will blow their freshness into you, and the storms their energy, while cares will drop off like falling leaves. (John Muir)

41

Directly after the Ice Age was the Age of Slush. (Sparrow)

In the long term, the economy and the environment are the same thing. If it's un-environmental, its un-economical. That is the rule of nature. (Mollie Beattie)

Humankind--despite its artistic pretensions, its sophistication, and its many accomplishments--owes its existence to a six-inch layer of topsoil and the fact that it rains.

It wasn't the *Exxon Valdez* captain's driving that caused the Alaskan spill. It was yours. (Greenpeace advertisement)

If we think of ourselves as coming out of the earth, rather than having been thrown in here from somewhere else, we see that we are the earth; we are the consciousness of the earth. These are the eyes of the earth. And this is the voice of the earth. (Joseph Campbell)

I do not know of a flowering plant that tastes good and is poisonous. Nature is not out to get you. (Euell Gibbons)

The sun shines not on us but in us. The rivers flow not past but through us, thrilling, tingling, vibrating every fiber and cell of the substance of our bodies, making them glide and sing. (John Muir)

We have to excel at one of two things. Either we become good at planting in the Spring, or we learn how to beg in the Fall. (Jim Rohn)

I have the world's largest collection of seashells. I keep it on all the beaches of the world. Perhaps you've seen it. (Steven Wright)

The earth laughs in flowers. (Ralph Waldo Emerson)

To the extent that most of us are users and consumers of energy and a certain style of life, we are covertly giving the go-ahead to our government to protect those things for us. We must realize that inherent in every time you turn on the ignition or climb into a jet plane, you are in some way part of a chain reinforcing six percent of the world that's using about fifty percent of its natural resources. And that's not fair. We can't play "King of the Mountain" much longer. We're not respected by any of the poor people of the world at this point, because our humanitarian concerns have been overridden by our fear of loss of our "King of the Mountain" status. (Ram Dass)

Until man duplicates a blade of grass, nature can laugh at his so-called scientific knowledge. Remedies from chemicals will never stand in favorable comparison with the products of nature, the living cell of the plant, the final result of the rays of the sun, the mother of all life. (Thomas Edison)

The average U.S. home contains more TVs than people. (Phil's Phunny Phacts)

Eating primarily what can be grown or preserved locally will definitely result in a more limited menu, but the food we do have will not only taste better and be more nutritious; it will also not carry the invisible price tag of environmental destruction and a huge carbon footprint. (Sandor Katz)

Prayer does not use up artificial energy, doesn't burn up any fossil fuel, doesn't pollute. Neither does song, neither does love, neither does the dance. (Margaret Mead)

One touch of nature makes the whole world kin. (William Shakespeare)

God has cared for these trees, saved them from drought, disease, avalanches, and a thousand tempests and floods. But he cannot save them from fools. (John Muir)

Nothing will benefit human health and increase chances for survival of life on earth as much as the evolution to a vegetarian diet. (Albert Einstein)

They paved paradise and put up a parking lot. (Joni Mitchell)

Every civilization reaches a moment of crisis. This crisis presents its challenge: smash or go on to higher things. So far no civilization has ever met this challenge successfully. History is the study of the bones of civilizations that failed, as the pterodactyl and the dinosaur failed. (Colin Wilson)

I am at two with nature. (Woody Allen)

Fall is my favorite season in Los Angeles, watching the birds change color and fall from the trees. (David Letterman)

The earth was small, light blue, and so touchingly alone, our home that must be defended like a holy relic. The earth was absolutely round. I believe I never knew what the word round meant until I saw the earth from space. (Russian cosmonaut Alexey Leonov)

Environment is Everything. (Bumper Sticker)

We do not inherit the earth from our ancestors; we borrow it from our children. (Native American Proverb)

It is not necessary to imagine the world ending in fire or ice. There are two other possibilities: one is paper work, and the other is nostalgia. (Frank Zappa)

EVERYDAY

I get up every morning determined both to change the world and to have one hell of a good time. Sometimes this makes planning the day difficult. (E.B. White)

There are no shortcuts to any place worth going. (Beverly Sills)

Silence is a source of great strength. (Lao Tzu)

Housework can't kill you, but why take a chance? (Phyllis Diller)

I hate housework! You make the beds, you do the dishes...and six months later you have to start all over again. (Joan Rivers)

No one really listens to anyone else, and if you try it for a while you'll see why. (Mignon McLaughlin)

Just 'cause you pour syrup on something doesn't make it pancakes. (Samuel L. Jackson)

The invariable mark of wisdom is to see the miraculous in the common. (Ralph Waldo Emerson)

Dogs got fleas and people got troubles. (Irene Hennessy-Willy's mom)

Do the kind of work during the day that allows you to sleep at night. (Amy Krouse Rosenthal's grandfather)

Never argue with a stupid person; they will drag you down to their level and then beat you with experience. (Mark Twain)

Any experience is better than no experience. (Chrissie Hynde of The Pretenders)

I'm officially changing my TV remote's name to Wally.

Vision is the art of seeing what is invisible to others. (Jonathan Swift)

When I buy a new book, I always read the last page first; that way, in case I die before I finish, I know how it ends. That, my friend, is a dark side. (Nora Ephron)

Every black American is bilingual. All of them. We speak street vernacular and we speak 'job interview.' (Dave Chappelle)

We made too many wrong mistakes. (Yogi Berra)

Common sense is genius dressed in its working clothes. (Ralph Waldo Emerson)

If I had nine of my fingers missing I wouldn't type any slower. (Mitch Hedberg)

Just bear this in mind, a true friend is hard to find,
So don't you mind people grinnin' in your face. (song lyric, Son House)

I am amazed at the strength my little finger can muster when my hands are full. (Aaron Karo-Ruminations.com)

What the world really needs is more love and less paperwork. (Pearl Bailey)

If you got something you don't want other people to know, keep it in your pocket. (Muddy Waters)

The less said, the better. (Jane Austen)

Judge not, that you be not judged. (New Testament, Matthew 7.1)

Dunbar's central ambition in life is to live as long as possible by making time pass as slowly as possible, which he does by cultivating boredom. (Joseph Heller, "Catch 22")

I work best with a gun at my head. (Coffee cup)

It has been my experience that folks who have no vices have very few virtues. (Abraham Lincoln)

When you doubt, abstain. (Ambrose Bierce)

It's the little things that smoothes people's roads the most. (Huck, in "The Adventures of Huckleberry Finn," Mark Twain)

There's no 'off' position on the genius switch. (David Letterman

If I had a nickel for every time I got distracted...Wow, I wish I had an ice cream cone.

It is wise to make a virtue of necessity. (Geoffrey Chaucer, William Shakespeare)

I decided to change calling the bathroom the "John" and renamed it the "Jim." I feel so much better saying I went to the Jim this morning.

When a true genius appears, you can know him by this sign: that all the dunces are in a confederacy against him. (Jonathan Swift)

Modesty is my best quality. (Jack Benny)

Nothing defines humans better than their willingness to do irrational things in the pursuit of phenomenally unlikely payoffs. This is the principle behind lotteries, dating, and religion. (Scott Adams, "Dilbert")

If you don't ask, the answer is always no. (Tony Robbins)

Life is the proper binge. (Julia Child)

A mind is like a parachute. It doesn't work if it is not open. (Frank Zappa)

Weather forecast for tonight: dark. (George Carlin)

For the most of life, nothing wonderful happens. If you don't enjoy getting up and working and finishing your work and sitting down to a meal with family or friends, then chances are that you're not going to be very happy. If someone bases his happiness or unhappiness on major events like a great new job, huge amounts of money, a flawlessly happy marriage, or a trip to Paris, that person isn't going to be happy much of the time. If, on the other hand, happiness depends on a good breakfast, flowers in the yard, a drink, or a nap, then we are more likely to live with quite a bit of happiness. (Andy Rooney)

TV or not TV. That is the question. (Lynn Joy "Tweakie" Kroeger)

I went to a garage sale. "How much for the garage?" "It's not for sale." (Steven Wright)

My apathy is at an all-time whatever.

I like to listen. I have learned a great deal from listening carefully. Most people never listen. (Ernest Hemingway)

Slow but steady wins the race. (Aesop)

Luck is being ready. (Brian Eno)

Recipe for Irish Rabbit Stew: First, catch the rabbit.

No one has ever said on their deathbed, "Gee, I wish I had spent more time alone with my computer. (Danielle Berry)

The hardest thing about doing nothing is knowing when you're through. (Sid Schults)

Personally, I'm waiting for caller IQ. (Paula Poundstone)

A thief believes everybody steals. (E.W. Howe)

A bird in the hand is worth two in the bush.

Reality leaves a lot to the imagination. (John Lennon)

The time you enjoy wasting is not wasted time. (Bertrand Russell)

My mind has changed during the last twenty or thirty years. Now for many years I cannot endure to read a line of poetry. I have also almost lost my taste for pictures or music. My mind seems to have become a kind of machine for grinding general laws out of large collections of facts. If I had to live my life again, I would have made a rule to read some poetry and listen to some music at least once every week. The loss of these tastes is a loss of happiness. (Charles Darwin)

Good grammar skills is something in which I excel in.

Education is what you read in fine print; experience is what you get when you don't. (Pete Seeger)

Have you ever noticed? Anybody going slower than you is an idiot, and anyone going faster than you is a maniac. (George Carlin)

I used up all of my sick days, so I'm calling in dead.

Nobody ever died of a dirty house. (Helen Staneski)

Human reason has this peculiarity, that by its very nature it is compelled to ask questions that by its very nature it is unable to answer. (Immanuel Kant, *Critique of Pure Reason*)

Live by this credo: Have a little laugh at life and look around you for happiness instead of sadness. Laughter has always brought me out of unhappy situations. (Red Skelton)

Do all the good you can. By all the means you can. In all the ways you can. In all the places you can. At all the times you can. To all the people you can. As long as ever you can. (John Wesley)

FASHION

It is always better to be slightly undressed. (Coco Chanel)

Once you accept the universe as matter expanding into nothing that is something, wearing stripes with plaid comes easy. (Albert Einstein)

The well-dressed man is he whose clothes you never notice. (W. Somerset Maugham)

I base my fashion taste on what doesn't itch. (Gilda Radner)

Every generation laughs at the old fashions, but religiously follows the new.
(Henry David Thoreau)

She was what we used to call a suicide blonde...dyed by her own hand. (Saul Bellow)

1000 milliliters of wet socks=1 literhosen

Clothes make the man. Naked people have little or no influence on society. (Mark Twain)

There are three ways a man can wear his hair: parted, unparted or departed.

Fashions, after all, are only induced epidemics. (George Bernard Shaw)

Phyllis Diller's had so many facelifts, there's nothing left in her shoes. (Bob Hope)

Never wear polyester to a wiener roast.

Give a girl the right shoes, and she can conquer the world. (Marilyn Monroe)

Five words you never hear in Las Vegas..."Does this go with this?"

FOOD

Older people shouldn't eat health food. They need all the preservatives they can get. (Robert Orben)

One of the disadvantages of wine is that it makes a man mistake words for thoughts, (Samuel Johnson)

I went to a fancy French restaurant called "Deja Vu." The headwaiter said, "Don't I know you?" (Steven Wright)

I prefer Hostess fruit pies to pop-up toaster tarts because they don't require so much cooking. (Carrie Snow)

No more "Wine in the box." It's now "Cardbordeaux."

Fettucini Alfredo is Macaroni & Cheese for adults. (Mitch Hedberg)

You can think as much as you like but you will not invent anything better than bread and salt. (Russian Proverb)

If this is coffee, please bring me some tea; but if this is tea, please bring me some coffee. (Abraham Lincoln)

I went into a McDonald's yesterday and said, "I'd like some fries." The girl at the counter asked, "Would you like fries with that?" (Jay Leno)

Tomato Soup:
      4 packets ketchup
      2 plastic tubs half & half
      1 cup hot water
      salt & pepper

Canada is a country without a cuisine. When's the last time you went out for Canadian? (Mike Myers)

I believe that if life gives you lemons, you should make lemonade…and try to find somebody whose life has given them vodka, and have a party. (Ron White)

The Himalayan Sea Salt we just got says it was created 250 million years ago. Label says the expiration date is 2016. Guess they dug it up just in time. (Jeff Dunham)

My wife is such a bad cook, in my house we pray after the meal. (Rodney Dangerfield)

JLYBLY (License plate on red VW Bug)

A knife that cuts four loaves of bread at a time?…A four-loaf cleaver.

I bought some powdered water, but I don't know what to add to it. (Steven Wright)

A book never written: "Healthy Foods," by Chris P. Bacon.

Wine is light, held together by water. (Galileo)

Red meat is not bad for you. Now blue-green meat, that's bad for you. (Tommy Smothers)

Everything I eat has been proved by some writer or another to be deadly poison. Everything I don't eat has been proved indispensable to life…but I go on marching. (George Bernard Shaw)

I had to go on two diets at once…I wasn't getting enough food on just one.

I put instant coffee in a microwave and almost went back in time.

This girl said she recognized me from the vegetarian club, but I'd never met herbivore. (Punography)

Men like to barbeque. Men will cook if danger is involved. (Rita Rudner)

The biggest seller is cookbooks and the second is diet books…how not to eat what you've just learned how to cook. (Andy Rooney)

Shake and shake
The catsup bottle.
None will come
And then a lot'll.   (Richard Armour)

Nothing takes the taste out of peanut butter quite like unrequited love. (Charlie Brown, Charles Shultz)

(Sign above a scale in a doctor's office) Pretend it's your I.Q.

Appetite is the best sauce. (French Proverb)

Stress cannot exist in the presence of pie. (David Mamet)

Equal amounts of dark chocolate and white chocolate make a balanced meal. (M. D. Rosenberg)

Chocolate-covered raisins, cherries, orange slices and strawberries all count as fruit…so eat as much as you want. (M. D. Rosenberg)

I'm on a diet where you eat everything you want and pray for a miracle.

Mushrooms always grow in damp places; is that why they look like umbrellas?

A McDonald's "Breakfast for Under a Dollar" actually costs much more than that. You have to factor in the cost of coronary-bypass surgery. (George Carlin)

I went to a restaurant with a sign that said they served breakfast at any time. So I ordered French toast during the Renaissance. (Steven Wright)

What do they plant to grow seedless grapes? (Bill Keane, "Family Circus")

You better cut the pizza in four pieces because I'm not hungry enough to eat six. (Yogi Berra)

Bacon is, like, meat candy.

Avoid cutting yourself when slicing vegetables by getting someone else to hold the vegetables while you chop.

There's a new garlic diet around. You don't lose weight, but you look thinner from a distance. (Red Shea)

A chain of Elvis Presley steak houses appeals to diners who love meat tender.

If I'd known I was gonna live this long, I'd have taken better care of myself. (Eubie Blake, pianist and composer. 1883-1983)

I enjoy cooking with wine; sometimes I even put it in the food I'm cooking. (Julia Child)

We ought to have a diet salad dressing called "500 Island." (George Carlin)

I'm on a grapefruit diet...I eat everything except grapefruit.

Why does Sea World have a seafood restaurant? I'm halfway through my fish burger and I realize, "Oh my God...I could be eating a slow learner." (Lynda Montgomery)

Microwaves need a "Melt Cheese" option. (Aaron Caro's Ruminations.com)

"Dunlop's Disease"...When your belly done lopped over your belt.

If you don't chew your food, who will? (Sign on restaurant wall, Oakland, California)

If you are what you eat, I'm dead meat.

The second day of a diet is always easier than the first. By the second day, you're off it. (Jackie Gleason)

Life is like a doughnut. You're either in the dough or in the hole.

Where do you go to get anorexia? (Shelley Winters)

I really don't think I need buns of steel. I'd be happy with buns of cinnamon. (Ellen DeGeneres)

A great new diet ...you can eat ANYTHING YOU WANT...but you have to eat it sitting around with naked fat people.

Health nuts are going to feel stupid someday, lying in hospitals dying of nothing. (Redd Foxx)

Ham and eggs...A day's work for a chicken, a lifetime commitment for a pig.

The most important part of any meal is someone to eat it with.

The Japanese eat little fat and suffer fewer heart attacks than the British or Americans. The French eat a lot of fat and also suffer fewer heart attacks than the British and Americans. The Italians drink a lot of red wine and they, too, suffer fewer heart attacks than the British or Americans. Conclusion: Eat and drink whatever you like...speaking English is apparently what kills you.

Can vegetarians eat animal crackers?

Jokes about German sausage are the wurst. (Punography)

Scientists are now saying that obesity can be caused by viruses. I guess you have to eat a lot of them. (Gregg Siegel)

The horse and mule live 30 years
    And nothing know of wines or beers.
The goat and sheep at 20 die
    And never taste of scotch or rye.
The cow drinks water by the ton
    And at 18 is mostly done.
The dog at 15 cashes in
    Without the aid of rum or gin.
The cat in milk and water soaks
    And then in 12 short years it croaks.
The modest, sober, bone-dry hen

Lays eggs for nogs, then dies at 10.
All animals are strictly dry;
    They sinless live and swiftly die;
But sinful, ginful, rum-soaked men
    Survive for three score years and ten.
And some of them, a very few,
    Stay pickled till they're 92.

Never eat more than you can lift. (Miss Piggy)

If people were not meant to have late night snacks, why did God put a light in the refrigerator?

A boiled egg is hard to beat.

Your body is your current address. (Tom Newbill)

The Donger needs food. ("Sixteen Candles," John Hughes)

I think children learning to cook can be such a wonderful thing. It can help build confidence, make them feel good about themselves. It helped me build my ego and even start to get acceptance at school. I'd bring things to class that I'd cooked at home. (Giada De Laurentiis)

I'm on a 60-day diet. So far I've lost 45 days. (Minerva Schurke)

Money talks. Chocolate sings.

Health food makes me sick. (Calvin Trillin)

Only Irish coffee provides, in a single glass, all four essential food groups: alcohol, caffeine, sugar and fat. (Alex Levine)

If a vegetarian eats vegetables, what does a humanitarian eat?

I opened a box of animal crackers, but there was nothing inside. They'd eaten each other. (Lily Tomlin)

I don't even butter my bread. I consider that cooking. (Katherine Cebrian)

I use a smoke alarm as a timer. (Carol Siskind)

1. Open fridge. Nothing to eat.
2. Open pantry. Nothing to eat.
3. Lower standards and repeat. (Aaron Karo's Ruminations.com)

Honey is said to be the only food that doesn't spoil.

I never feel lonely in the kitchen. Food is very friendly. (Julia Child)

They say exercise and a proper diet are the keys to a longer life. Oh, well. (Drew Carey)

I can make the phone ring just by shoving the last oversized bite of burger into my mouth.

The way a sauce can redeem a meal is unique to the culinary arts. You can't pour a liquid over an essay and make it suddenly successful. (Sparrow, Sun magazine)

I stand holding the apple in both hands. It feels precious, like a heavy treasure. I lift it up and smell it. It has such an odor of outdoors on it I want to cry. (Margaret Atwood)

The four basic food groups:
    1) Fast
    2) Frozen
    3) Take-out
    4) Delivered

How to trap fruit flies:
Place a small bowl on the counter. Put enough apple cider vinegar to cover bottom of bowl. Cover with plastic wrap (tight) secure with rubber band. Poke tiny holes (with toothpick) in top of plastic wrap. Flies get in and can't get out!

If you ate pasta and antipasto, would you still be hungry? (Steven Wright)

An apple pie without some cheese is like a kiss without a squeeze.

Everything you see I owe to Spaghetti. (Sophia Loren)

C U 4 T (License plate)

HOLIDAYS

Aren't we forgetting the true meaning of Christmas? You know, the birth of Santa. (Bart Simpson)

Darth Vader: Luke Skywalker, I know what you're getting for Christmas.
Luke: How do you know?
Vader: I felt your presents

Nothing says holidays like a cheese log. (Ellen DeGeneres)

Labor Day is a holiday honoring those who work for a living. Laborious Day is a lesser-known holiday honoring those who cannot stop talking about their work. (Lemony Snicket)

I bought my brother some gift wrap for Christmas. I took it to the gift wrap department and told them to wrap it, but in a different print so he would know when to stop unwrapping. (Steven Wright)

Thanksgiving: when the Indians said, "Well, this has been fun, but we know you have a long voyage back to England. (Jay Leno)

I celebrated Thanksgiving in an old-fashioned way. I invited everyone in my neighborhood to my house, we had an enormous feast, and then I killed them and took their land. (Jon Stewart)

Oh, for the good old days when people would stop Christmas shopping when they ran out of money.

I once wanted to become an atheist, but I gave up...they have no holidays. (Henny Youngman)

Cooking Tip: Wrap turkey leftovers in aluminum foil and throw them out. (Nicole Hollander)

What do you get when you cross a bell with a skunk?...Jingle Smells.

JIVE & CHOPS

You look like a hundred bucks!

Here he is...the Van Gogh of music...he doesn't have an ear.

So long, King Kong.

I have not the pleasure of understanding you. (Jane Austen)

Good thinkin,' Lincoln.

And now, here he is, the poster boy for birth control. (Rodney Dangerfield)

You're a neo maxi zoom dweebie. (John Hughes)

You're just like good wine...You should be locked in a cellar.

Is that your face or did your pants fall down?

You need a check-up from the neck up.

He is not only dull himself; he is the cause of dullness in others. (Samuel Johnson)

Lester Young was playing one night with a drummer he really didn't like. The drummer kept on trying to be friendly all night; he finally trapped Lester at the bar after the gig was over, saying, "I sure had a good time tonight, Pres...I've been thinking, when was the last time we worked together?" Lester's answer..."Tonight!"

How many polyesters were killed to make that suit?

Is that your head or did your neck throw up? (Tom Waits)

I'd like to help you out...which way did you come in?

You look tired...have you been thinking?

Did your mother have any children who lived?

Do they ever shut up on your planet?

He had delusions of adequacy. (Walter Kerr)

He has all the virtues I dislike and none of the vices I admire. (Winston Churchill)

He has no enemies, but is intensely disliked by his friends. (Oscar Wilde)

He loves nature in spite of what it did to him. (Forrest Tucker)

I'd love to chat but I gotta scat.

Let's play "Horse." I'll be the front end...you just be yourself.

I'm writing a term paper on jerks...May I interview you?

You guessed'er, Chester.

Somebody school that fool!

Ain't nothin' but a party!

Stick out your cans...here comes the garbage man.

Don't kill that half pint!

Put down that racing form and pay attention! (Louis Jordan)

Give me a huge break, one time!

We're lookin' like home cookin.'

I hear you buzzin,' cousin!

On your mark; get set; go away!

Some cause happiness wherever they go; others, *when*ever they go. (Oscar Wilde)

Hi...my answering machine is out of order...this is Willy speaking.

I've had a perfectly wonderful evening. But this wasn't it. (Groucho Marx)

I see your IQ tests were negative.

What's steamin,' Demon?

Plant you now and dig you later.

Did you heard me?!

How it is?

You're baloney without the mayo. (Frank Zappa)

If I don't see you in the future, I'll see you in the pasture. (Tom Newbill)

I'll check you now and cash you later. (Craig Buhler)

KID JOKES

What did the sushi say to the bee?..."Wa-SAA-bee?"

What do you get when you cross a dinosaur with a pig?...Jurassic Pork. (Madison)

What kind of underclothes do clouds wear? ...Thunderpants!

What's red and smells like blue paint?...Red paint.

Who eats at underwater restaurants?...SCUBA diners.

Why did the hot dog lose the race?...He couldn't ketchup. (Ellery)

Where does the Easter bunny get his breakfast?...IHOP. (Nicole)

Is a Hippopotamus a Hippopotamus, or a really cool Opotamus? (Mitch Hedberg)

Why couldn't the teddy bear finish his dinner?...He was stuffed.

Which side of the turkey has the most feathers?...The outside.

What did the astronaut cook in his skillet?...Unidentified Frying Objects.

How do you fix a broken pumpkin?...With a pumpkin patch.

What do you call a sleeping bull?...A bulldozer. (Gavin)

What kind of shoes do frogs wear?...Open toad. (Ireneusz)

What do you call an alligator in a vest?...An investigator. (Caroline)

What is large, gray, and wears glass slippers? ...Cinderelephant.

Why does Piglet smell so bad?...He always plays with Pooh.

What's a tree's favorite drink?...Root Beer! (Nicole, 6)

What do you get when you cross a duck and a rooster?...A duck that gets up at the quack of dawn! (Jack, 10)

Why did the apple take out a fig?...Because he couldn't find a date. (Faith, 9)

Girl: Why do elephants paint their toenails red?
Boy: I don't know.
Girl: So they can hide in cherry trees.
Boy: I've never seen an elephant in a cherry tree.
Girl: See, it works!

What's an astronaut's favorite meal?...Launch!

What did the ocean say to the sky?...Nothing. It just waved. (John)

What lives underwater and loves peanut butter and jelly sandwiches?...A peanut butter and jelly fish.

What birds always stick together?...Vel crows. (Caroline)

How would you feel if you ate 100 pancakes?...Just waffle.

Why should you never fly with Peter Pan?...Because you'll never, never land.

Knock, knock.
Who's there?
Hatch.
Hatch who?
Are you catching a cold?

Why was six afraid of seven?...Because seven eight nine.

BFLY XXS (License plate)

A bicycle can't stand alone because it is two-tired.

What is H, I, J, K, L, M, N, O?...The formula for water: H to O (H2O). (Jeremy)

What is the biggest pencil in the world?...Pennsylvania. (Marine)

What's the 44th President's favorite vegetable? ...Barackoli. (Lochtyn)

What has a head and a tail but no body?...A coin. (Shreya)

What do you call a fish with no eyes?...A f sh.

What is a vampire's favorite fruit?...Nectarine.

What do you call a vampire who lives in the kitchen? ...Spatula! (Megan)

What do you get when you cross an elephant and a fish?...Swimming trunks. (Lindsey)

What goes 'ooooo'?...a cow with no lips.

What do you get when you cross a snowman and a vampire?...Frostbite.

What did one volcano say to the other volcano?...I lava you. (Mark)

What kind of music do mummies like most?...Wrap.

Why are spiders good baseball players?...They are good at catching flies. (Andrew)

What did the judge say when the skunk walked in?...Odor in the court! (Ryan)

Playing baseball alone in his backyard, a boy announced, "I'm the greatest hitter in the world!" He tossed the ball into the air, swung hard, and missed. "Strike one!" he yelled. He picked up the ball and said again, "I'm the greatest hitter in the world!" Feeling confident this time, he lobbed the ball, swung...and missed. "Strike two!" he yelled. The boy examined his bat and then his ball. He spit on his hands, rubbed them together, then tugged his cap and repeated, "I'm the greatest hitter in the world!" Again he tossed the ball, swung and missed. "Wow!' the boy exclaimed. "I'm the greatest pitcher in the world!"

What kind of keys don't work?...Monkeys and donkeys. (Griffin)

What runs faster, hot or cold?...Hot, anyone can catch a cold. (Brennen)

What building has the most stories?...The Library. (Robert)

What did the squash wear to the beach?...A zucchini. (Samantha)

What songs do the planets sing?...Neptunes. (Caroline)

Why did the whale cross the road?...To get to the other tide.

What happens to frogs that park illegally?...They get toad.

What kind of animal shouldn't you play cards with?...A cheetah. (Ann)

When is a door not a door?...When it's ajar. (Joey)

A young boy enters a barber shop and the barber whispers to his customer,
'This is the dumbest kid in the world. Watch while I prove it to you.'
The barber puts a dollar bill in one hand and two quarters in the other, then calls the boy over and asks, *'Which do you want, son?'*
The boy takes the quarters and leaves the dollar.
'What did I tell you?' said the barber. *'That kid never learns!'*
Later, when the customer leaves, he sees the same young boy coming out of the ice cream store & says ;
'Hey, son! May I ask you a question? Why did you take the quarters instead of the dollar bill?'
The boy licked his ice cream cone and replied, *'Because the day I take the dollar, the game's over!'*

What do you get when you cross a bear with a skunk?...Winnie-the-P U. (Alfred)

Why did the chicken cross the playground?...To get to the other slide. (Gabriela)

I was going to look for my watch, but I could never find the time. (Sean)

What do you call cheese that is not yours?...Nacho cheese. (Sydney)

How much do monkeys like bananas?...A bunch.

What do you call a boomerang that doesn't come back?...A stick. (Chris)

GOOD YOUTUBE VIDEO..."Read a Book by Sarah Brady"

MEDICINE

I had amnesia once or twice. (Steven Wright)

Everything that used to be a sin is now a disease. (Bill Maher)

The worst time to have a heart attack is during a game of charades. (Demetri Martin)

I read somewhere that 77 per cent of all the mentally ill live in poverty. Actually, I'm more intrigued by the 23 per cent who are apparently doing quite well for themselves. (Jerry Garcia, The Grateful Dead)

Let your food be your medicine. (Hippocrates)

New support group for compulsive talkers: On and On Anon.

Dyslexics have more fnu.

When you get a bladder infection, urine trouble. (Punography)

Splinter remover: duct tape.

An early-morning walk is a blessing for the whole day. (Henry David Thoreau)

I was going to have cosmetic surgery until I noticed that the doctor's office was full of portraits by Picasso. (Rita Rudner)

It is part of the cure to wish to be cured. (Seneca)

I drive way too fast to worry about cholesterol. (Steven Wright)

There is no medicine like hope.

What disease did cured ham actually have?

Smoking cures weight problems...eventually. (Steven Wright)

England has no kidney bank, but it does have a Liverpool. (M. D. Rosenberg)

Beer is a gateway drug to aspirin.

I recently went to a new doctor and noticed he was located in something called the "Professional Building." I felt better right away. (George Carlin)

Each patient ought to feel somewhat the better after the physician's visit, irrespective of the nature of the illness. (Warfield Theobald Longcope)

I didn't make to the gym today. That makes five years in a row.

An apple a day keeps the doctor away. What will an onion do?...Keep everyone away.

Thousands upon thousands of persons have studied disease. Almost no one has studied health. (Adelle Davis)

Never go a doctor whose office plants have died. (Erma Brombeck)

I'm addicted to placebos. I'd give them up, but it wouldn't make any difference. (Jay Leno)

INNIE (Audi license plate)

There is one thing that the medical profession cannot do and that is save people from being idiots. (Craig Ferguson)

I've got a wonderful doctor. If you can't afford the operation, he touches up the X-rays. (Henny Youngman)

I went to the psychiatrist, and he says, "You're crazy." I tell him I want a second opinion. He says, "Okay, you're ugly too!" (Rodney Dangerfield)

I told my psychiatrist that everyone hates me. He said I was being ridiculous...everyone hasn't met me yet. (Rodney Dangerfield)

Last week I told my psychiatrist, "I keep thinking about suicide." He told me from now on I have to pay in advance. (Rodney Dangerfield)

Last week I saw my psychiatrist. I told him, "Doc, I keep thinking I'm a dog." He told me to get off his couch. (Rodney Dangerfield)

The pain-relieving ingredient...there's always got to be a lot of that. Nobody wants anything less than extra-strength. "Give me the maximum allowable human dosage. Figure out what will kill me, and then back it off a little bit." (Jerry Seinfeld)

First the doctor told me the good news: I was going to have a disease named after me. (Steve Martin)

Isn't it a bit unnerving that doctors call what they do "practice"? (George Carlin)

Reading is to the mind what exercise is to the body. (Joseph Addison)

A lot of people are afraid of heights. Not me, I'm afraid of widths. (Steven Wright)

If you have a bad cough, take a large dose of laxatives. Then you'll be afraid to cough.

My doctor said I looked like a million dollars...green and wrinkled. (Red Skelton)

A sure cure for seasickness is to sit under a tree. (Spike Milligan)

I took some Nyquil and NoDoze at the same time. I had a dream that I couldn't sleep. (Steven Wright)

They told me I had Type A blood, but it was a Type O.

Be careful about reading health books. You may die of a misprint. (Mark Twain)

When the doctor is 45 minutes late for your appointment, you understand why they call us "patients." (Dave Cross)

The chief cause of stress is reality. (Lily Tomlin)

Be kind to your dentist. He has fillings too.

Edible plants protect people. And what are they protecting them from? Obesity, diabetes, heart disease, and cancer. (Alison Ashton)

A man visits his doctor after weeks of not feeling well.
"I have bad news," says the doctor. "You don't have long to live."
"How long have I got?" asks the distraught man.
"Ten," the doctor says sadly.
"Ten? Ten what? Months? Days?
The doctor interrupts, "nine...eight..."

MONEY

Money frees you from doing things you dislike. Since I dislike doing nearly everything, money is handy. (Groucho Marx)

Less is the new more.

Not getting behind is the new getting ahead. (Charlie Hunter CD title)

Always borrow money from a pessimist. He won't expect it back.

If you buy the farm, you get the pigs.

Due to current financial constraints, the light at the end of the tunnel will be turned off until further notice.

(Talking about television) If we were to do the Second Coming of Christ in color for a full hour, there would be a considerable number of stations which would decline to carry it on the grounds that a Western or a quiz show would be more profitable. (Edward R. Murrow)

If I had his money, I'd throw mine away. (Irene Hennessy-Willy's mom)

Gambling is a sure way of getting nothing for something. (Wilson Mizner)

A friend at school was always being laughed at because his father emptied dustbins for a living. But those who laughed worshipped famous footballers. This is an example of our topsy-turvy view of 'success.' Who would we miss most if they did not work for a month, the footballer or the garbage collector? (David Icke)

If you want to know what God thinks of money, just look at the people he gave it to. (Dorothy Parker)

At the bank, I told the cashier, "'I'd like to open a joint account please." "OK, with whom?" "Whoever has lots of money."

He who likes cherries soon learns to climb. (German proverb)

I'll keep it short and sweet. Family, Religion, Friendship. These are the three demons you must slay if you wish to succeed in business. (Montgomery Burns, The Simpsons)

Debt---An ingenious substitute for the chain and whip of the slave driver. (Ambrose Bierce)

Ahhhh, bad credit...the best identity theft protection. (Aaron Caro's Ruminations.com)

I just met Darth Vader's corrupt brother, Taxi Vader.

A wise man should have money in his head, but not in his heart. (Jonathan Swift)

Nothing is so hard for those who abound in riches as to conceive how others can be in want. (Jonathan Swift)

Inflation hasn't ruined everything. A dime can still be used as a screwdriver. (Quoted in P.S. I Love You, compiled by H. Jackson Brown, Jr.)

I'm underpaid and worth every penny of it.

Money talks---but credit has an echo. (Bob Thaves)

All I ask is the chance to prove that money can't make me happy. (Spike Milligan)

Nothing is worth more than this day. (Goethe)

I'm thankful for the three-ounce Ziploc bag, so that I have somewhere to put my savings. (Paula Poundstone)

If you fear change, leave it here. (Sign on a restaurant tip jar)

Everybody needs money. That's why they call it *money*. (Danny De Vito in "Heist" (2001), screenplay by David Mamet)

8 nickels=2 paradigms

I spent most of my money on women and drink and like a fool I squandered the rest. (Benny Hill)

There is nobody in this country who got rich on their own. Nobody. You built a factory out there…good for you. But I want to be clear. You moved your goods to market on the roads the rest of us paid for. You hired workers the rest of us paid to educate. You were safe in your factory because of police forces and fire forces that the rest of us paid for. You didn't have to worry that marauding bands would come and seize everything at your factory…Now look. You built a factory and it turned into something terrific or a great idea…God bless! Keep a big hunk of it. But part of the underlying social contract is you take a hunk of that and pay it forward for the next kid who comes along. (Elizabeth Warren)

I bet you I could stop gambling.

A study of economics reveals that the best time to buy anything is last year. (Whit Stillman)

The two most beautiful words in the English language are "check enclosed." (Dorothy Parker)

One must be poor to know the luxury of giving. (George Eliot)

I figure you have the same chance of winning the lottery whether you play or not. (Fran Lebowitz)

I'm as broke as the Ten Commandments. (Terry Robb)

There's something about getting up at 5 AM, feeding the stock and chickens, and milking a couple of cows before breakfast that gives you a lifelong respect for the price of butter and eggs. (William E. Vaughan)

The lack of money is the root of all evil. (Mark Twain)

A rich man is nothing but a poor man with money. (W.C. Fields)

There are 293 ways to make change for a dollar.

I am having an out-of-money experience.

Dealer: "19."
Homer: "Hit me!"
Dealer: "20."
Homer: "Hit me!"
Dealer: "21."
Homer: "Hit me!"
Dealer: "22."
Homer: "D'oh!"
(The Simpsons)

Honesty is the best policy...when there is money in it. (Mark Twain)

So long as there's a jingle in your head, television isn't free. (Jason Love)

It's not that it's so good with money, but that it's so bad without it. (George Sanders)

If your outgo exceeds your income, your upkeep will be your downfall.

Someday I want to be rich. Some people get so rich they lose all respect for humanity. That's how rich I want to be. (Rita Rudner)

Money buys privacy, silence. The less money you have, the noisier it is; the thinner your walls, the closer your neighbors. The first thing you notice when you step into the house or apartment of a rich person is how quiet it is. (Fran Lebowitz)

If advertisers spent the same amount of money on improving their products as they do on advertising, then they wouldn't have to advertise them. (Will Rogers)

I'd like to live as a poor man with lots of money. (Pablo Picasso)

The quickest way to double your money is to fold it and put it back in your wallet. (Will Rogers)

Few of us can stand prosperity. Another man's, I mean. (Mark Twain)

I had plastic surgery last week...I cut up my credit cards. (Henny Youngman)

I have enough money to last me the rest of my life, unless I buy something. (Jackie Mason)

The time to save is now. When a dog gets a bone, he doesn't go out and make a down payment on a bigger bone. He buries the one the he's got. (Will Rogers)

I've got the Midas touch...everything I touch turns into a muffler.

Nothing incites to money-crimes like great poverty or great wealth. (Mark Twain)

You can fool some of the people some of the time...and that's enough to make a decent living. (W.C. Fields)

The most precious thing we have is life, yet it has absolutely no trade-in value.

Two can live as cheaply as one...for half as long. ("Back To Broke")

Some people are born on third base and go through life thinking they hit a triple.

Let's go Dutch...you pay and I'll wear wooden shoes.

If Wal-Mart is lowering prices every day, how come nothing is free yet?

Money doesn't always bring happiness. People with ten million dollars are no happier than people with nine million dollars. (Hobart Brown)

Money's like manure...It doesn't do any good unless you spread it around.

The Income Tax has made liars out of more Americans than golf. (Will Rogers)

That's the way it goes…first your money, then your clothes. (Irene Hennessy, Willy's mom)

Credit is a system whereby a person who cannot pay gets another who cannot pay to guarantee that he can pay. (Charles Dickens)

I started out with nothing, and I've managed to hold on to most of it.

They say money talks; well, mine just says "Goodbye."

Formula for success: rise early, work hard, strike oil. (J. Paul Getty)

I was walking down Fifth Avenue today, and I found a wallet. I was going to return it, rather than keep it, but I thought: Well, if I lost $150, how would I feel? And I realized I would want to be taught a lesson. (Emo Philips)

There are two slaves in a consumer society: the prisoners of envy, and the prisoners of addiction. (Ivan Illich)

If a parsley farmer is sued, do they garnish his wages?

During the contest for the 1961 Democratic presidential nomination, John F. Kennedy visited a mine in West Virginia. "Is it true you're the son of one of our wealthiest men?" asked one of the miners there. Kennedy admitted that this was true. "Is it true that you've never wanted for anything and had everything you wanted?" "I guess so," Kennedy replied. "Is it true you've never done a day's work with your hands all your life?" Kennedy nodded. "Well, let me tell you this," said the miner. "You haven't missed a thing. (Bartlett's Book of Anecdotes)

How come the rich people have all the money? (Red Skelton)

Despite the cost of living, have you noticed how it remains so popular?

In order to get a loan, you must first prove you don't need it.

A college diploma is just a big fancy receipt. (Aaron Karo)

So you think that money is the root of all evil? Have you ever asked what is the root of money? (Ayn Rand)

I've been rich and I've been poor. Rich is better. (Sophie Tucker)

Billionaires pay a lower tax rate than their secretaries. Does anyone have a problem with that? (Elizabeth Warren)

Some people think they are worth a lot of money just because they have it. (Fannie Hurst)

Money often costs too much. (Ralph Waldo Emerson)

What's the use of happiness? It can't buy you money. (Henny Youngman)

When you go to work, if your name is on the building, you're rich. If your name is on your desk, you're middle-class. If your name is on your shirt, you're poor. (Rich Hall)

Money is better than poverty, if only for financial reasons. (Woody Allen)

Too many people spend money they haven't earned to buy things they don't want to impress people they don't like. (Will Rogers)

Where the hell is "Easy Street?"

It isn't what a man has that constitutes wealth. No...it is to be satisfied with what one has; that is wealth. (Mark Twain)

MOVING ON

When I die, I'm going to leave my body to science fiction. (Steven Wright)

My only regret in life is that I wasn't born somebody else. (Woody Allen)

Average age is when you stop criticizing the old and start criticizing the young. (L.J. Peter)

Two babies were born on the same day at the same hospital. They lay there and looked at each other. Their families came and took them away. Eighty years later, by a bizarre coincidence, they lay in the same hospital, on their deathbeds, next to each other. One of them looked at the other and said, "So. What did you think?" (Steven Wright)

Half our life is spent trying to find something to do with the time we have rushed through life trying to save. (Will Rogers)

Live every day like it's your last, 'cause one day you're gonna be right. (Ray Charles)

Just before the funeral services, the undertaker came up to the very elderly widow and asked, "How old was your husband?"
"98," she replied: "Two years older than me"
"So you're 96," the undertaker commented.
She responded, "Hardly worth going home, is it?"

No one comes back from the dead, no one has entered the world without crying; no one is asked when he wishes to enter life, nor when he wishes to leave. (Soren Kierkegaard)

My memory's not as sharp as it used to be. Also, my memory's not as sharp as it used to be.

Old age is the most unexpected of all things that can happen to a man. (Trotsky)

They say such nice things about people at their funerals that it makes me sad to realize I'm going to miss mine by just a few days. (Garrison Keillor)

We're on vacation now. (Tom Newbill)

These days, my happy hour is a nap.

We are here to laugh at the odds and live our lives so well that Death will tremble to take us. (Charles Bukowski)

It's not length of life, but depth of life. (Ralph Waldo Emerson)

You must learn some of my philosophy. Think only of the past as its remembrance gives you pleasure. (Jane Austen)

I plan to live forever. So far so good. (Will Brady)

I'll tell you how to stay young: Hang out with older people. (Bob Hope)

Life moves pretty fast. If you don't stop and look around once in a while, you could miss it. (John Hughes)

Wine improves with age. The older I get, the better I like it.

When it comes time to die, make sure all you got to do is die. (Jim Elliot)

If you continue to work and to absorb the beauty in the world around you, you will find that age does not necessarily mean getting old. (Pablo Casals at 93)

Enjoy every sandwich. (Warren Zevon)

You should always go to other people's funerals; otherwise, they won't come to yours. (Yogi Berra)

A person is always startled when he hears himself seriously called an old man for the first time. (Oliver Wendell Holmes Sr.)

I look forward to being older, when what you look like becomes less and less an issue and what you are is the point. (Susan Sarandon)

All goes onward and outward, nothing collapses. And to die is different from what anyone supposed, and luckier. (Walt Whitman)

Father Time is undefeated. (Lebron James)

I'm gonna live forever, or die trying. (Joseph Heller, "Catch 22")

What do you call somebody who's happy on Monday?...Retired. (Ron Trulock)

Three friends die in a car accident, and they go to an orientation in heaven. They are all asked, "When you are in your casket and friends and family are mourning you, what would you like to hear them say about you?"
The first guy says, "I would like to hear them say that I

was a great doctor in my time and a great family man."
The second guys says, "I would like to hear that I was a
wonderful husband and a school teacher who made a
huge difference in our children of tomorrow."
The last guy replies, "I would like to hear them
say...'Look, he's moving'!!"

I usually take a two-hour nap from one to four. (Yogi
Berra)

If I am ever stuck on a respirator or a life-support
system, I definitely want to be unplugged...but not until I
get down to a size eight. (Henriette Mantel)

The dying process begins the minute we are born, but it
accelerates during dinner parties. (Carol Matthau)

How old would you be if you didn't know how old you
was? (Satchel Paige)

Life is short, but it's wide. (Jim Gordon)

They always told me when I was young, "Just wait, and
you'll see." Now I'm old and see nothing. It's wonderful.
(Erik Satie)

I have a terrible memory; I never forget a thing. (Edith
Konecky)

Jiddu Krishnamurti, one of the most revered spiritual
teachers of this century, once asked a small group of
listeners what they would say to a close friend who is
about to die. Their answers dealt with assurances, words
about beginnings and endings, and various gestures of
compassion. Krishnamurti stopped them short. "There is
only one thing you can say to give the deepest comfort,"
he said. "Tell them that in his death a part of you dies

and goes with him. Wherever he goes, you go also. He will not be alone." (Larry Dossey)

Of the five most important things in life, health is first, knowledge is second and wealth is third. I forgot the other two. (Chuck Berry)

"My cousin just died. He was only 19. He got stung by a bee...the natural enemy of a tightrope walker." (Dan Rather, former news anchorman)

Life is pleasant. Death is peaceful. It's the transition that's troublesome. (Isaac Asimov)

I don't know what it means to be mortal, but I'm pretty sure it's not a compliment. (Woody Allen)

We don't grow older, we grow riper. (Pablo Picasso)

Reporter interviewing a 104-year-old woman: What do you think is the best thing about being 104?
Woman: No peer pressure. (Sylvia R. Shiner)

A man was telling his neighbor, "I just bought a new hearing aid. It cost me four thousand dollars, but it's state of the art."
"Really," answered the neighbor. "What kind is it?"
"Twelve thirty."

I'm not lying: Reaching 50 meant a lot to me. For starters, it meant I wasn't dead. (George Lopez)

I don't plan to grow old gracefully. I plan to have facelifts until my ears meet. (Rita Rudner)

The tragedy of old age is not that one is old, but that one is young. (Oscar Wilde)

"When I turned two I was really anxious, because I'd doubled my age in a year. I thought, "If this keeps up, by the time I'm six, I'll be ninety." (Steven Wright)

I'd rather be dead than singing "Satisfaction" when I'm forty-five. (Mick Jagger in a 1975 interview. Mick still performs the song at seventy. Dig it. It's still a good song.)

When I die I want to go peacefully, like my grandfather did…in his sleep. Not screaming like the passengers in his car.

I have never killed a man, but I have read many obituaries with great pleasure. (Clarence Darrow)

I didn't attend the funeral, but I sent a nice letter saying I approved of it. (Mark Twain)

There is a fountain of youth; it is your mind, your talents, the creativity you bring to your life and the lives of the people around you. When you will learn to tap this source, you will have truly defeated age. (Sophia Loren)

I intend to live forever or die trying. (Groucho Marx)

Some people, no matter how old they get, never lose their beauty…they merely move it from their faces into their hearts. (Martin Baxbaum)

I don't like to work out. Whenever I get the urge to exercise, I lie down until it passes. (Al Pacino)

On a grave in East Dalhousie Cemetery, Nova Scotia: Here lies Ezekial Aikle, Age 102, The Good Die Young.

Wine is old men's milk.

"Let us be kinder to one another." Aldous Huxley's last words.

Oscar Wilde's last words on his dying bed: "Either this wallpaper goes, or I go."

Grandchildren are God's way of compensating us for growing old. (Mary H. Waldrip)

Doctor: "You're in great shape for a sixty year old."
Patient: "Who says I'm sixty years old?"
Doctor: "You're not sixty? How old are you?"
Patient: "I turn eighty next month."
Doctor: "Gosh, eighty! Do you mind if I ask you at what age your father died?"
Patient: "Who says my father's dead?"
Doctor: "He's not dead?"
Patient: "Nope, he'll be 104 this year."
Doctor: "With such a good family medical history your grandfather must have been pretty old when he died."
Patient: "Who says my grandfather's dead?"
Doctor: "He's not dead?!"
Patient: "Nope, he'll be 129 this year, and he's getting married next week."
Doctor: "Unbelievable! Why at his age would he want to get married?"
Patient: "Who says he wants to?"

Age is a case of mind over matter. If you don't mind, it don't matter. (Satchel Paige)

I had a friend who was a clown for the Ringling Brothers circus, and when he died, all his friends went to the funeral in one car. (Steven Wright)

You are never too old to be what you might have been. (George Eliot)

My grandmother started walking five miles a day when she was sixty. She's ninety-three today, and we don't know where the hell she is. (Ellen DeGeneres)

Death twitches my ear. "Live," he says. "I am coming." (Virgil)

If you were going to die soon and had only one phone call you could make, whom would you call and what would you say? And why are you waiting? (Stephen Levine)

After his annual physical examination, an elderly patient asked the doctor, "Tell me, how long am I going to live."
"Don't worry," his doctor replied. "You'll probably live to be eighty."
"But Doctor, I *am* eighty," he said.
"See? What did I tell you?"

Birthdays are good for you; the more you have, the longer you live.

The doctors x-rayed my head and found nothing. (Dizzy Dean)

We all have our time machines. Those that take us back are memories, and those that take us forward are dreams. (H.G. Wells)

If Shaw and Einstein couldn't beat death, what chance have I got?...Practically none. (Mel Brooks)

We could certainly slow the aging process down if it had to work its way through Congress. (Will Rogers)

There are worse things in life than death. Have you ever spent an evening with an insurance salesman? (Woody Allen)

Do you think we should drive a stake through his heart just in case? (Peter Lorre to Vincent Price at Bela Lugosi's funeral)

Even in the valley of the shadow of death, two and two do not make six. (Leo Tolstoy)

Death is the cure for all diseases. (Thomas Browne)

If my doctor told me I only had six minutes to live, I wouldn't brood. I'd type a little faster. (Isaac Asimov)

In life, unlike in chess, the game continues after checkmate. (Isaac Asimov)

I would like to be remembered as someone who was extremely old. (Jim Davis-creator of "Garfield")

MUSIC DICTIONARY

A PATELLA: Unaccompanied knee-slapping.

ACCIDENTALS: Wrong Notes

ADAGIO FROMMAGIO: To play in a slow and cheesy manner.

AGNUS DEI: A famous female church composer

ALLEGRO: Leg fertilizer

ANGUS DEI: To play with a divine, beefy tone.

CADENCE: When everybody hopes you're going to stop, but you don't.

CHROMATIC SCALE: An instrument for weighing that indicates half-pounds.

DA CAPO AL FINE: I like your hat.

DIATONIC: A low calorie Schweppes.

DILL PICCOLINO: A wind instrument that plays only sour notes.

FRUGALHORN: A sensible, inexpensive brass instrument.

HARMONY: A corn-like food, popular in the South.

INTERVAL: How long it takes you to find the right note.

INTONATION: Singing through one's nose.

MEAN TEMPERAMENT: One's state of mind when everybody's trying to tune at the same time.

METRONOME: A dwarf that lives in the city.

MUSICIAN: Someone who puts $5,000 worth of gear into a $500 car to drive 100 miles to a $50 gig.

TEMPO: This is where a headache begins.

TEMPO DE LEARNO: As slow as you have to go. (Dave Cross)

Yogi Berra explains "Jazz":
Interviewer: Can you explain jazz?
Yogi: I can't, but I will....90% of all jazz is half improvisation. The other half is the part people play while others are playing something they never played with anyone who played that part. So if you play the

wrong part, its right. If you play the right part, it might be right if you play it wrong enough. But if you play it too right, it will be wrong.

Interviewer: I don't think I quite understand.

Yogi: Anyone who understands jazz knows that you can't understand it. It's too complicated. That's what's so simple about it.

Interviewer: So, do you understand it?

Yogi: No. That's why I can explain it. If I understood it, I wouldn't know anything about it.

Interviewer: Are there any great jazz players still alive today?

Yogi: No. All the great jazz players alive today are dead, except for the ones that are still alive. But so many of them are dead, that the ones that are still alive are dying to be like the ones that are dead. Some would kill for it.

Interviewer: What is syncopation?

Yogi: That's when the note that you should hear, now happens either before or after you hear it. In jazz, you don't hear notes when they happen, because that would be some other type of music. Other types of music can be jazz, but only if they're the same as something different from those other kinds.

Interviewer: Now I really don't understand. I'm really confused!

Yogi: I haven't taught you enough for you to not understand jazz that well.

A Shepard Tone, named after Roger Shepard, is a sound consisting of a superposition of sine waves separated by octaves. When played with the base pitch of the tone moving upwards or downwards, it is referred to as the Shepard scale. This creates the auditory illusion of a tone that continually ascends or descends in pitch, yet which ultimately seems to get no higher or lower.

(From the bandstand) Knock, knock.
Who's there?
Wilbur Wright.
Wilbur Wright who?
Wilber Wright back after a break!

Testing, I, IV, V. (Will Brady)

Bandleader after a break: "When I called a ten minute break, I meant fifteen minutes, not twenty."

Note Names of the Guitar Strings (Standard Tuning):
Low to High: E-A-D-G-B-E
"Eddie Ate Dynamite, Good Bye Eddie"

OPTIMISM

Behind the cloud the sun is still shining. (Abraham Lincoln)

The average pencil is seven inches long, with just a half-inch eraser...in case you thought optimism was dead. (Robert Brault)

Against the assault of laughter, nothing can stand. (Mark Twain)

I have never met a man so ignorant that I couldn't learn something from him. (Galileo Galilei)

Pessimism is for wimps. (Jaron Lanier)

I have a dream that my four little children will one day live in a nation where they will not be judged by the color of their skin, but by the content of their character. (Martin Luther King)

I tried to catch some fog. I mist. (Punography)

It's a helluva start, being able to recognize what makes you happy. (Lucille Ball)

The sun don't shine on the same dog every day. (Song lyric, Richard Stekol)

A bird does not sing because it has an answer, it sings because it has a song. (Maya Angelou)

My barn having burnt down, I could now see the moon. (D. Deubelbeiss)

Won't you come into the garden? I would like my roses

to see you. (Richard B. Sheridan)

Martin Luther King Jr. once said, "Let us realize the arc of the moral universe is long, but it bends toward justice." This metaphorical framework has a long history that stretches back to the 19th century. Theologian Theodore Parker in 1853: "Look at the facts of the world. You see a continual and progressive triumph of the right. I do not pretend to understand the moral universe, the arc is a long one, my eye reaches but little ways. I cannot calculate the curve and complete the figure by the experience of sight; I can divine it by conscience. But from what I see I am sure it bends towards justice."

I don't panic when I get lost. I just change where I want to go. (Rita Rudner)

The heart that loves is always young. (Greek Proverb)

The nice part about being a pessimist is that you are constantly being either proven right or pleasantly surprised. (George Will)

"Thou shalt love the Lord thy God with thy whole heart, with thy whole soul, and with thy whole mind." This is the commandment of the great God, and He cannot command the impossible. Love is a fruit in season at all times, and within reach of every hand. Anyone may gather it and no limit is set. Everyone can reach this love through meditation, spirit of prayer, and sacrifice, by an intense inner life. (Mother Theresa)

The optimist proclaims that this is the best of all possible worlds. The pessimist fears this is true.

If you can't be a good example, then you'll just have to be a horrible warning.

An optimist is a person who starts a new diet on Thanksgiving Day. (Harold Helfer)

If you observe a really happy man, you'll find him building a boat, writing a symphony, educating his son, growing double dahlias in his garden. He will not be searching for happiness as if it were a collar stud that has rolled under the dressing table. (W. Beran Wolfe)

What a wonderful life I've had. I only wish I'd realized it sooner. (Collette)

Experience is that marvelous thing that enables you to recognize a mistake when you make it again. (Franklin P. Jones)

Each man takes care that his neighbor shall not cheat him. But a day comes when he begins to care that he does not cheat his neighbor. Then all goes well. He has changed his market-cart into a chariot of the sun. (Ralph Waldo Emerson)

I'm not old...I'm chronologically gifted.
I'm not bald...I'm just taller than my hair.
I'm not fat...I'm just short for my weight.

I'm an optimistic pessimist. I look forward to thinking the worst.

The grand show is eternal. It is always sunrise somewhere; the dew is never all dried at once; a shower is forever falling; vapor is ever rising. Eternal sunrise, eternal dawn and gloaming, on sea and continents and islands, each in its turn, as the round earth rolls. (John Muir)

The world is round and the place which may seem like

the end may also be only the beginning. (Ivy Baker Priest)

Our true nationality is mankind. (H. G. Wells)

Nothing is foolproof to the sufficiently talented fool.

He's turned his life around. He used to be depressed and miserable. Now he's miserable and depressed. (David Frost)

I love to sleep. It really is the best of both worlds. You get to be alive and unconscious. (Rita Rudner)

A cynic is a man who, when he smells flowers, looks around for a coffin. (H.L. Mencken)

There is a wonderful mystical law of nature that the three things we crave most in life--happiness, freedom, and peace of mind--are always attained by giving them to someone else.

Oh, you hate your job? Why didn't you say so? There's a support group for that. It's called EVERYBODY, and they meet at the bar. (Drew Carey)

Recall it as often as you wish, a happy memory never wears out. (Libbie Fudim)

Everywhere is within walking distance if you have the time. (Steven Wright)

It's tough to make predictions, especially about the future. (Yogi Berra)

A well-adjusted person is one who makes the same mistake twice without getting nervous. (Alexander Hamilton)

I've learned to take vacations 15 minutes at a time. (Dave Cross)

Even a blind squirrel gets an acorn once in a while. (Jim Sullivan)

Hard work has a future payoff. Laziness pays off now.

I ran out of ice cream bars the other day, and I cried. Then I remembered Alexander the Great, and how he wept when there were no more worlds to conquer. How very much alike we are, I thought.

PARENTS

As a child, my family's menu consisted of two choices: Take it or leave it. (Buddy Hackett)

I got my sense of humor from my parents...That's why they don't have one anymore. (Wendy Liebman)

Our children give us the opportunity to become the parents we always wished we had. (Louise Hart)

No matter how old you are, if a little kid hands you a toy phone...you answer it. (Dave Chappelle)

I want my children to have all the things I couldn't afford. Then I want to move in with them. (Phyllis Diller)

SGR SPCE (License plate)

Most of us become parents long before we have stopped being children. (Mignon McLaughlin)

My mom and I have always been really close. She's always been the friend that was always there. There were times when, in middle school and junior high, I didn't have a lot of friends. But my mom was always my friend. Always. (Taylor Swift)

In general, my children refused to eat anything that hadn't danced on TV. (Erma Bombeck)

Push your children in the direction that they already want to go. (Dave Cross)

Until I was thirteen, I thought my name was SHUT UP. (Joe Namath)

The first thing a child should learn is how to endure. It is what he will have most need to know. (Jean-Jacques Rousseau)

It is easier to build strong children than to repair broken men. (Fredrick Douglass)

When you have teenagers, it's important to have a dog so that someone in the house is happy to see you. (Nora Ephron)

Children need love, especially when they do not deserve it. (Harold S. Hulbert)

I can take a fifteen-minute nap in fifteen minutes. (Beth Fitchet Wood, at that time a new mom)

I'm not going to buy my kids an encyclopedia. Let them walk to school like I did. (Yogi Berra)

A parent is only as happy as their saddest child. (Tom Newbill)

We spend the first twelve months of our children's lives teaching them to walk and talk and the next twelve years telling them to sit down and shut up. (Phyllis Diller)

I could tell my parents hated me. My bath toys were a toaster and a radio. (Rodney Dangerfield)

You don't really understand human nature unless you know why a child on a merry-go-round will wave at his parents every time around…and why his parents will always wave back. (William D. Tammeus)

KDSNPTS (License plate station wagon with back in disarray)

I grew up with six brothers. That's how I learned to dance...waiting for the bathroom. (Bob Hope)

There is no such thing as fun for the whole family. (Jerry Seinfeld)

You can learn many things from children. How much patience you have, for instance. (Franklin P. Adams)

Isn't "Bonus mom" better than "Step mom?"

If you want your children to improve, let them overhear the nice things you say about them to others. (Haim Ginott)

It goes without saying that you should never have more children than you have car windows. (Erma Bombeck)

A child's life is like a piece of paper on which every person leaves a mark. (Chinese Proverb)

There are no college courses to build up self-esteem, or high school or elementary school classes. If you don't get those values at an early age, nurtured in your home, you don't get them. (T. D. Jakes)

What's it like to be a baby? It's like being in love in Paris for the first time after you've had three double espressos. (Alison Gopnik)

If there is a hell, it is modeled after junior high. (Lewis Black)

I like children. Fried. (W.C. Fields)

Police were called to a day care center, where a 3-year-old was resisting a rest.

Silence is golden, duct tape is silver.

My parents took me to Amish country, to see a bunch of people that have no cars, no TV, no phone. Who wants to see a whole community that's been grounded? (Jerry Seinfeld)

Children today are tyrants. They contradict their parents, gobble their food, and tyrannize their teachers. (Socrates, 400 BC)

Turning the other cheek is all well and good, but Jesus was neither married nor a parent. (Molly Maslin Arbogast)

I have found the best way to give advice to your children is to find out what they want and then advise them to do it. (Harry S. Truman)

I cheat my boys every chance I get. I want to make 'em sharp. I trade with the boys and skin 'em and I just beat 'em every time I can. (William Rockefeller, father of John D. Rockefeller)

A baby is God's opinion that life should go on.

Never will a time come when the most marvelous recent invention is as marvelous as a newborn baby. The finest of our precision watches, the most super-colossal of our supercargo planes don't compare with a newborn baby in the number and ingenuity of coils and springs, in the flow and change of chemical solutions, in timing devices and interrelated parts that are irreplaceable. (Carl Sandburg)

The way I feel, if the kids are still alive when my husband comes home from work, I've done my job. (Roseanne Barr)

I told my mother-in-law that my house was her house, and she said, "Get the hell off my property." (Joan Rivers)

Having a family is like having a bowling alley installed in your head. (Martin Mull)

Somewhere on this globe every ten seconds, there is a woman giving birth to a child. She must be found and stopped. (Sam Levenson)

Parents often talk about the younger generation as if they didn't have anything to do with it. (Haim Ginott)

If your parents never had children, chances are you won't either. (Dick Cavett)

Too many people grow up. They don't remember what it's like to be twelve years old. They patronize; they treat children as inferiors. Well, I won't do that. (Walt Disney)

When I was a little kid we had a sand box. It was a quicksand box. I was an only child...eventually. (Steven Wright)

Children lack morality, but they also lack fake morality. (Mignon McLaughlin)

When I was born, I was so surprised I couldn't talk for a year and a half. (Gracie Allen)

Human beings are the only creatures that allow their children to come back home.

My mother said, "You won't amount to anything because you procrastinate." I said, "Just you wait." (Judy Tenuta)

A two-year-old is like a blender without the top on. (Jerry Seinfeld)

Even very recently, the elders could say [to the youths]: "You know, I have been young and you have never been old." But today's young people can reply: "You have never been young in the world that I am young in, and you never can be."...This break between generations is wholly new: it is planetary and universal. (Margaret Mead)

The simplest toy, one which even the youngest child can operate, is called a grandparent. (Sam Levenson)

Each generation has been an education for us in different ways. The first child, with bloody nose, was rushed to the emergency room. The fifth child, with bloody nose, was told to go to the yard immediately and stop bleeding on the carpet. (Art Linkletter)

The most important thing a father can do for his children is to love their mother. (Theodore Hesburgh)

Ask your child what he wants for dinner only if he's buying. (Fran Lebowitz)

Once a parent, always a parent. (Tom Shaver)

PARTNERS

"Where's home for you?" a stranger asks a fellow traveler on a plane. "Wherever she is," comes the reply, as the man points to his wife.

The Eskimos had fifty-two names for snow because it was important to them: there ought to be as many for love. (Margaret Atwood)

4MYRGNA (License plate)

No matter what kind of backgrounds two men are from, if you go, "Hey, man, women are crazy," you've got a friend. (Chris Rock)

Behind every great man is a woman rolling her eyes. (Jim Carrey)

Shared joy is double joy, and shared sorrow is half-sorrow. (Swedish proverb)

You can't make old friends.

Some people ask the secret of our long marriage. We take time to go to a restaurant two times a week. A little candlelight, dinner, soft music, and dancing. She goes Tuesdays, I go Fridays. (Henny Youngman)

The secret of a happy marriage?...Do what your wife tells you!" (Denzel Washington)

A million light years and a million more / would not give time enough to store / that small second of eternity / when I took you in my arms / and you took me in yours. (Jacques Prevert)

We are not the same persons this year as last; nor are those we love. It is a happy chance if we, changing, continue to love a changed person. (W. Somerset Maugham)

Our marriage license turned out to be a learner's permit. (Joan Rivers)

Keep your eyes wide open before marriage, half-shut afterwards. (Benjamin Franklin)

In my house I'm the boss, my wife is just the decision maker. (Woody Allen)

No, I don't understand my husband's theory of relativity, but I know my husband and I know he can be trusted. (Elsa Einstein)

Those that have loved longest love best. (Samuel L. Jackson)

In a Westways Magazine interview Robert De Niro was asked: "When traveling, is there anything special you always carry with you?" (points to his wedding ring) "This."

I used to believe that marriage would diminish me, reduce my options. That you had to be someone less to live with someone else, when, of course, you have to be someone more. (Candice Bergen)

My wife just asked, "What's that pile of clothes doing on the bathroom floor?" I said, "It's a dead Jedi."

My wife Mary and I have been married for forty-seven years and not once have we had an argument serious enough to consider divorce; murder, yes, but divorce, never. (Jack Benny)

Divorce is possibly as old as marriage. Although I suppose that marriage is several weeks older. (Voltaire)

It takes two to quarrel, but only one to end it. (Spanish proverb)

A kiss is a lovely trick designed by nature to stop speech when words become superfluous. (Ingrid Bergman)

Thelonius Monk's wife called him "Melodious Thunk."

Marriage is our last, best chance to grow up. (Joseph Barth)

The most effective way to remember your wife's birthday is to forget it once. (Ogden Nash)

Bigamy is having one husband too many. Monogamy is the same. (Erica Jong)

You can't stay mad at somebody who makes you laugh. (Jay Leno)

Never ruin an apology with an excuse. (Benjamin Franklin)

I am a marvelous housekeeper. Every time I leave a man I keep his house. (Zsa Zsa Gabor)

How many husbands have I had? You mean apart from my own? (Zsa Zsa Gabor)

The only way to have a friend is to be one. (Ralph Waldo Emerson)

A woman's heart beats faster than a man's.

Love is blind but marriage is a real eye opener.

Selfishness is not living as one wishes to live; it is asking others to live as one wishes to live. (Oscar Wilde)

Women don't want to hear what you think. Women want to hear what they think, in a deeper voice.

Bob read a newspaper story about an actress who'd married an athlete known for his low IQ. He turned to his wife, Mona, and asked, "Why is it that the biggest dolts end up with the most attractive wives?" Mona touched his hand. "Why, thank you, dear," she said.

SWTEPI (License plate)

And they lived happily (aside from a few normal disagreements, misunderstandings, pouts, silent treatments, and unexpected calamities) ever after. (Jean Ferris)

The most dangerous food is wedding cake. (James Thurber)

My neighbor and his wife get along well considering it's a mixed marriage...She's normal. (Mike Melfi)

Gravitation cannot be held responsible for people falling in love. (Albert Einstein)

Why are women wearing perfumes that smell like flowers? Men don't like flowers. I've been wearing a great scent. It's called New Car Interior. (Rita Rudner)

The kindest word in the world is the unkind word, unsaid.

My wife and I had words, but I didn't get to use mine.

A married couple, both 60 years old, were celebrating their 35th anniversary. During their party, a fairy appeared to congratulate them and grant them each one wish. The wife wanted to travel around the world. The fairy waved her wand and *poof*—the wife had tickets in her hand for a world cruise. Next, the fairy asked the husband what he wanted. He said, "I wish I had a wife 30 years younger than me." So the fairy waved her wand and *poof*—the husband was 90.

The first duty of love…is to listen. (Paul Tillich)

Young son: "Is it true, dad, I heard that in some parts of Africa a man doesn't know his wife until he marries her?" Dad: "That happens in every country, son."

According to a new survey, women say they feel more comfortable undressing in front of men than they do undressing in front of other women. They say that women are too judgmental, whereas, of course, men are just grateful. (Robert De Niro)

Water runs thicker than blood
Under the bridge of a troubled love. (song lyric, Sue Cross)

For one human being to love another: that is perhaps the most difficult of all our tasks; the ultimate, the last test and proof, the work for which all other work is but preparation. (Rainer Maria Rilke)

A happy marriage is the union of two forgivers. (Ruth Bell Graham)

The whole trade in the luxuries of life is brought into existence and supported by the requirements of women. (Leo Tolstoy)

Accept me as I am...only then will we discover each other. (Federico Fellini's 8 ½)

There are two theories to arguing with a woman...Neither works. (Will Rogers)

The best proof of love is trust. (Joyce Brothers)

It's easy to halve the potato where there's love. (Irish Proverb)

Nothing makes us feel so strong as a call for help. (George MacDonald)

A friend will help you move. A really good friend will help you move a body.

Love is or it ain't. Thin love ain't love at all. (Toni Morrison, "Beloved")

According to 'Modern Bride' magazine, the average bride spends 150 hours planning her wedding. The average groom spends 150 hours going, "Yeah, sounds good." (Jay Leno)

I'm not upset about my divorce. I'm only upset I'm not a widow. (Roseanne Barr)

A faithful friend is the medicine of life. (The Bible)

People change and forget to tell each other. (Lillian Hellman)

And then there was the male spotted owl who told his wife, "What do you mean you have a headache? We're an endangered species!" (John Bunzel)

The secret of a happy marriage remains a secret.
(Henny Youngman)

They say married men live longer. It just seems longer.
(Bobby Slayton)

Humor is the shortest distance between two people.
(Victor Borge)

I had a rose named after me and I was very flattered.
But I was not pleased to read the description in the
catalog: 'No good in a bed, but fine against a wall.'
(Eleanor Roosevelt)

To the world you may be one person, but to one person
you may be the world. (Heather Cortez-seen in "Mutts")

"I Love You" in 8 languages:
English-I Love You
Spanish-Te Amo
French-Je T'aime
German-Ich Liebe Dich
Japanese-Ai Shite Imasu
Italian-Ti Amo
Chinese-Wo Ai Ni
Swedish-Jag Alskar

I was married by a judge. I should have asked for a jury.
(Groucho Marx)

An elderly man was stopped by the police around 2 AM
and was asked where he was going at that time of night.
The man replied, "I'm on my way to a lecture about
alcohol abuse and the effects it has on the human body,
as well as smoking, and staying out late." The officer
then asked, "Really? Who's giving that lecture at this
time of night?" The man replied, "That would be my
wife."

Marriage is very difficult. Marriage is like a 5,000-piece jigsaw puzzle, all sky. (Cathy Ladman)

All men make mistakes, but married men find out about them sooner. (Red Skelton)

Any man who drives safely while kissing a pretty girl is simply not giving the kiss the attention it deserves. (Albert Einstein)

The penalty for bigamy: two wives.

PEP TALK

Start every day with a smile and get it over with. (W. C. Fields)

Life has two rules: Number one, never quit; Number two, always remember rule number one. (Duke Ellington)

Be happy. It's one way of being wise. (Collette)

As a cure for worrying, work is better than whiskey. (Ralph Waldo Emerson)

Courage can't see around corners but goes around them anyway. (Mignon McLaughlin)

Before everything else, getting ready is the secret of success. (Henry Ford)

People say, "One day we'll look back on this and laugh." I say, "Why wait?" (Fran Solomon)

He who mounts a wild elephant goes where the wild elephant goes. (Randolph Bourne)

Knowledge is complex, specific, learned; Wisdom is simple, general, intuitive. Discernment applies wisdom and knowledge to a moment; Resolve generates action in that moment. That's the formula for right action: wisdom, knowledge, discernment, resolve. (Dave Cross)

If you don't know where you are going, you might wind up someplace else. (Yogi Berra)

Goals are only wishes unless you have a plan. (Melinda Gates)

Goals are dreams with deadlines. (Diana Scharf Hunt)

None of us will ever accomplish anything excellent or commanding except when he listens to this whisper which is heard by him alone. (Ralph Waldo Emerson)

Live like a mighty river. (Buddha)

If anything is worth trying at all, it's worth trying at least ten times. (Art Linkletter)

We are always more anxious to be distinguished for a talent which we do not possess, than to be praised for the fifteen which we do possess. (Mark Twain)

Did you ever stop to think, and forget to start again? (Winnie the Pooh)

I hate advice unless I'm giving it. (Jack Nicholson)

XROADS (License plate)

Whatever you are, be a good one. (Abe Lincoln)

I can rise and shine. But not at the same time.

Be yourself. Everyone else is taken. (Barry Pearl)

If trying harder doesn't work, try softer. (Lily Tomlin)

The man with a new idea is a Crank until the idea succeeds. (Mark Twain)

Fall seven times, stand up eight. (Japanese saying)

Laziness is merely the habit of resting before you're tired.

A journey of a thousand miles begins with a single step. (Lao-Tzu)

Someone's boring me. I think it's me. (Dylan Thomas)

If no one ever took risks, Michelangelo would have painted the Sistine floor. (Neil Simon)

The only way to know how much is enough, is to do too much, and then back up. (Jerry Jeff Walker)

Walk away from it until you're stronger. All your problems will be there when you get back, but you'll be better able to cope. (Lady Bird Johnson)

Live each day like it's your second-to-last. That way you can fall asleep at night. (Jason Love)

Glory is fleeting, but obscurity is forever. (Napoleon Bonaparte)

As my late father always said, "get a decent watch."

Be a first-rate version of yourself, not a second-rate version of someone else. (Judy Garland)

Do or watch. (Joseph Baldassare)

After twelve years of therapy my psychiatrist said something that brought tears to my eyes: "No hablo Ingles." (Ronnie Shakes)

It's hard to beat a person who never gives up. (Babe Ruth)

I am a nobody, nobody is perfect, therefore, I am perfect.

Life is something like this trumpet. If you don't put anything in it, you don't get anything out. (W. C. Handy)

Opportunity's favorite disguise is trouble.

It's a shallow life that doesn't give a person a few scars. (Garrison Keillor)

You hit or you sit. (McMurphy in "One Flew Over the Cuckoo's Nest.")

Talk doesn't cook rice. (Chinese Proverb)

Worry does not empty tomorrow of its sorrow, it empties today of its joy.

One may go a long way after one is tired. (French Proverb)

We cannot do everything at once, but we can do something at once. (Calvin Coolidge)

To finish first you must first finish. (Rick Mears, retired race car driver)

I am always ready to learn, although I do not always like to be taught. (Winston Churchill)

Luge strategy? Lie flat and try not to die. (Carmen Boyle-Olympic Luge Gold Medal winner, 1996)

If you come to a fork in the road…take it. (Yogi Berra)

Negative results are just what I want. They're just as valuable to me as positive results. I can never find the thing that does the job best until I find the ones that don't. (Thomas Edison)

Failure is the opportunity to begin again more intelligently. (Henry Ford)

It's amazing what you don't get when you don't ask. (Berney Neufield)

The way to get started is to quit talking and begin doing. (Walt Disney)

It doesn't work to leap a twenty-foot chasm in two ten-foot jumps.

If you want your dreams to come true, don't sleep. (Yiddish proverb)

I went to a bookstore and asked the sales woman, "Where's the self-help section?" She said if she told me, it would defeat the purpose.

A good plan today is better than a perfect plan tomorrow.

If you ever need a helping hand, you'll find one at the end of your arm. (Yiddish proverb)

On the whole, human beings want to be good, but not too good, and not quite all the time. (George Orwell)

All opinion is transient, and all work is permanent. (Man Ray)

Shallow men believe in luck, believe in circumstance. Strong men believe in cause and effect. (Ralph Waldo Emerson)

It's never too late to be what you might have been. (George Eliot)

Life is a riddle. Unfortunately, the answer's not written on the back of anything.

It takes a rare person to want to hear what they don't want to hear. (Dick Cavett)

There are two types of people in the world, good and bad. The good sleep better, but the bad seem to enjoy the waking hours much more. (Woody Allen)

God gives the nuts, but He does not crack them. (German Proverb)

I miss 100% of the shots I don't take. (Wayne Gretsky)

Talk is cheap because supply exceeds demand.

There never was a good knife made of bad steel. (Benjamin Franklin)

It's a sad dog that can't wag its' own tail. (Benjamin Franklin)

Fear nothing, for every renewed effort raises all former failures into lessons, all sins into experiences. (Katherine Tingley)

The day after tomorrow is the third day of the rest of your life. (George Carlin)

Who is more foolish: the child afraid of the dark or the man afraid of the light? (Maurice Freehill)

Nobody who gave their best ever regretted it.

Smooth seas do not make skillful sailors. (African proverb)

I do not take drugs...I *am* drugs. (Salvador Dali)

Don't aim at the bull's-eye, aim at the center of the bull's-eye.

Nobody's born a bigot.

Procrastinate now. Don't put it off. (Ellen DeGeneres)

In a moment of decision, the best thing to do is the right thing to do. The worst thing to do is nothing. (Theodore Roosevelt)

Experience is something you get just after you need it.

The difference between a smart man and a wise man is that the smart man knows what to say, and a wise man knows whether or not to say it.

Think twice...speak once. (Howlin' Wolf)

The harder I work, the luckier I get.

If you're going through hell, keep going. (Winston Churchill)

I don't know the key to success, but the key to failure is trying to please everybody.

Never miss a good chance to shut up. (Will Rogers)

Life is tricky. (Barry Kagan)

Two kinds of people fail—those who listen to nobody, and those who listen to everybody.

The "Rule of Holes"...If you are in one, stop digging.

Those are my principals. If you don't like them I have others. (Groucho Marx)

I have found that if you love life, life will love you back. (Arthur Rubinstein)

I personally think we developed language because of our deep inner need to complain. (Jane Wagner)

A loving heart is the truest wisdom. (Charles Dickens)

The best way out of a difficulty is through it. (Will Rogers)

Be kind, for everyone you meet is fighting a hard battle. (Plato)

A point in every direction is no point at all. (Harry Nielson)

When I work, I relax; doing nothing makes me tired. (Pablo Picasso)

When you come to the edge of all the light you have and must take a step into the darkness of the unknown, believe that one of two things will happen. Either there will be something solid for you to stand on—or you will be taught how to fly. (Patrick Overton)

A man only learns in two ways: one by reading, and the other by association with smarter people. (Will Rogers)

You'll never have all the information you need to make a decision. If you did, it would be a foregone conclusion, not a decision.

There's nothing quite so satisfying as being shot at and missed.

You must keep your mind on the objective, not on the obstacle. (William Randolph Hearst)

Luck is when preparation meets opportunity.

Time is the coin of your life. It is the only coin you have, and only you can determine how it will be spent. Be careful lest you let other people spend it for you. (Carl Sandburg)

Whether you think you can or think you can't, you're right in both cases.

When you don't know what you're talking about, it's hard to know when you're finished. (Tom Smothers)

Not everybody can be famous but everybody can be great because greatness is determined by service. (Martin Luther King)

To hell with the advances in computers; *You* are supposed to advance and become, not the computers. Find out what's inside you...and don't kill anybody. (Kurt Vonnegut)

Nothing is easy to the unwilling.

Just remember, we're all in this alone. (Lily Tomlin)

Advice is what we ask for when we already know the answer but wish we didn't. (Erica Jong)

Work is a necessity for man. Man invented the alarm clock. (Pablo Picasso)

It's kind of fun to do the impossible. (Walt Disney).

If you don't practice you don't deserve to win. (Andre Agassi)

If you think you are too small to be effective, you have never been in bed with a mosquito. (Bette Reese)

No matter what people tell you, words and ideas can change the world. (Robin Williams)

Life shrinks or expands according to one's courage. (Anais Nin)

Hard work pays off in the future. Laziness pays off now.

Try? There is no try. There is only do or not do. (Yoda, "The Empire Strikes Back")

Whenever I feel blue, I start breathing again.

I never learned anything while I was talking. (Larry King)

Always remember that you are absolutely unique...just like everyone else. (Margaret Mead)

Action is the antidote to despair. (Joan Baez)

If there is no wind, row. (Latin Proverb)

The future does not equal the past. (Tony Robbins)

I'm an idealist. I don't know where I'm going but I'm on my way. (Carl Sandburg)

Nothing can substitute for just plain hard work. (Andre Agassi)

A new idea is rarely born like Venus attended by graces.
More commonly it's modeled of bailing wire and acne.
More commonly it wheezes and tips over. (Marge
Piercy)

Formula for success: rise early, work hard, strike oil.
(John Paul Getty)

If you can take it, you can make it.

Nunc Coepi...."Now I Begin." Latin, pronounced "noonk
CHEPee." (San Diego Chargers "Mantra")

A closed mouth gathers no flies. ("My Left Foot")

You've got to take the bitter with the sour. (Samuel
Goldwyn)

Always slow down for Dead Man's Curve.

POETRY

If called by a panther
    don't anther (Ogden Nash)

An operatic tenor named Boyce
    shattered fine mirrors with his voice
At a party with class
he broke all the glass
    and rode home in a windy Rolls Royce

One, two, three
    Buckle my shoe (Robert Benchley)

A tutor who tooted the flute
    Tried to tutor two tooters to toot
Said the two to the tutor
"Is it harder to toot, or
    to tutor two tooters to toot?"

Roses are red
    Violets are blue
I'm schizophrenic
    And so am I (Oscar Levant)

Life is hard
    by the yard
But by the inch
    life's a cinch (Jean Gordon)

When you're kissing with your honey
    And your nose feels runny
You may think it's funny
    But it's not

I don't give a damn for a man that can only spell a word
one way. (Mark Twain)

You have brains in your head
   You have feet in your shoes
You can steer yourself
   Any direction you choose (Dr. Seuss)

C-D-E-D-B-D ducks?
      M-R-not ducks!
O-S-A-R
      C-D-E-D-B-D wings?

Thoidy doidy boids
      Sittin' on da coib
Choipin' 'n boipin'
      N' eatin' doidy oith woims
Along comes Hoibie
      From Thoidy-thoid 'n Thoid
Saw da thoidy doidy boids
      Sittin' on da coib
Choipin' 'n boipin'
      N' eatin' doidy oith woims
Boy...was he distoibed   (The Red Hot Chili Peppers)

There once was a girl named Sarah
Who, at twenty, was really quite fair-ah
But even more nifty
As a girl of fifty
Blossomed with beauty most rare-ah (Willy)

The trouble with a kitten is
THAT
Eventually it becomes a
CAT (Ogden Nash)

A wonderful bird is the pelican.
His mouth can hold more than his belican.
He can take in his beak
Enough food for a week
I'm darned if I know how the helican. (Dixon L. Merritt)

130

POLITICS & HISTORY

I think we ought to make "America the Beautiful" the national anthem. It's not about war, there's no bombs bursting in air, no rocket's red glare. It's about the land, amber waves of grain. That sounds good to me. Plus, it's a hell of a lot easier to sing. (Willie Nelson)

Politics is the entertainment division of the military-industrial complex. (Frank Zappa)

The Second Amendment says we have the right to bear arms, not to bear artillery. (Robin Williams)

The enemy is anybody who's going to get you killed, no matter which side he's on. (Joseph Heller, "Catch 22")

You can fool too many of the people too much of the time. (James Thurber)

A fool and his money are soon elected. (Will Rogers)

A politician is a statesman who approaches every question with an open mouth. (Adlai Stevenson)

All I say is, kings is kings, and you got to make allowances. Take them all around, they're a mighty ornery lot. It's the way they're raised. (Huck, in "The Adventures of Huckleberry Finn," Mark Twain)

As I would not be a slave, so I would not be a master. This expresses my idea of democracy. Whatever differs from this, to the extent of the difference, is no democracy. (Abraham Lincoln)

Thomas Jefferson believed that Americans should revisit the Constitution every 20 years and rewrite it from scratch, that "The earth belongs to the living, and not to the dead."

Injustice anywhere is a threat to justice everywhere. (Martin Luther King)

Never forget that everything Hitler did in Germany was legal. (Martin Luther King)

In the Soviet Union, capitalism triumphed over communism. In this country, capitalism triumphed over democracy. (Fran Lebowitz)

It used to be, everyone was entitled to their own opinion, but not their own facts. But that's not the case anymore. Facts matter not at all. Perception is everything. (Stephen Colbert)

If you wish to be a success in the world, promise everything, deliver nothing. (Napoleon)

The ballot is stronger than the bullet. (Abraham Lincoln)

What Washington needs is adult supervision. (Barack Obama)

True terror is to wake up one morning and discover that your high-school class is running the country. (Kurt Vonnegut)

The American Constitution was not written to protect criminals; it was written to keep the government from becoming criminals. (Lenny Bruce)

I like America, just as everybody else does. I love America, I gotta say that. But America will be judged. (Bob Dylan)

Everything is changing. People are taking musicians seriously and the politicians as a joke. (Will Rogers)

AF TWO (Lexus license plate)

131

Politics have no relation to morals. (Machiavelli)

A government that robs Peter to pay Paul can always depend on the support of Paul. (George Bernard Shaw)

Why were the Indians here first? They had reservations. (Punography)

I'm not a Republican…but I am saving up to be one. (Emo Philips)

The problem with political jokes is they get elected. (Henry Cate VII)

There's an old saying about those who forget history. I don't remember it, but it's good. (Stephen Colbert)

A feud is this way: A man has a quarrel with another man, and kills him; then that other man's brother kills him; then the other brothers, on both sides, goes for one another; then the cousins chip in -- and by and by everybody's killed off, and there ain't no more feud. But it's kind of slow, and takes a long time. (Huck, in "The Adventures of Huckleberry Finn," Mark Twain)

You don't pay taxes; they take taxes. (Chris Rock)

It depends on what your definition of "is," is. (Bill Clinton, then president, testifying, on camera, during impeachment hearings)

Even Napoleon had his Watergate. (Yogi Berra)

Did you see where eBay wouldn't let this guy auction off his soul? They said, "If you want to sell your soul, you'll just have to run for President like everybody else." (Jay Leno)

You can fool some of the people all of the time and all of the people some of the time, but you can`t fool all of the people all of the time. (Abraham Lincoln)

Nobody ever went broke underestimating the intelligence of the American people. (H. L. Mencken)

The greatest lesson in life is to know that even fools are right sometimes. (Winston Churchill)

The central question is whether the wonderfully diverse and gifted assemblage of human beings on this earth really knows how to run a civilization. (Adlai Stevenson)

Great wealth is its own Nationality. (Velda Johnston)

Whenever I hear anyone arguing for slavery, I feel a strong impulse to see it tried on him personally. (Abraham Lincoln)

Of all forms of tyranny the least attractive and the most vulgar is the tyranny of mere wealth, the tyranny of plutocracy. (Theodore Roosevelt)

The one thing that doesn't abide by majority rule is a person's conscience. (Harper Lee, "To Kill a Mockingbird")

Pit race against race, religion against religion, prejudice against prejudice. Divide and conquer! We must not let that happen here. (Eleanor Roosevelt)

Why do Americans choose from just two contenders for President, but fifty for Miss America?

If pro is the opposite of con, then what is the opposite of progress?

More than any other time in history, mankind faces the crossroads. One path leads to despair and utter hopelessness, the other to total extinction. I pray we have the wisdom to choose wisely. (Woody Allen)

The pen is mightier than the sword.

People sleep peaceably in their beds at night only because rough men stand ready to do violence on their behalf. (George Orwell)

Being powerful is like being a lady. If you have to tell people you are, you aren`t. (Margaret Thatcher)

I don't belong to any organized political party; I'm a Democrat. (Will Rogers)

The three branches of government: Financial, Petrochemical, and Pharmaceutical. (Bumper sticker)

Cruelty and fear shake hands together. (Honore de Balzac)

We have to face that either all of us are going to die together or we are going to learn to live together, and if we are to live together we have to talk. (Eleanor Roosevelt)

Did you know that a large group of baboons is called a congress? That explains a lot now, doesn't it? (Aaron Caro's Ruminations.com)

In the country of the blind, the one-eyed man is king.

Democracy is the worst form of government...except for all the others. (Winston Churchill)

We have the Bill of Rights. What we need is a Bill of Responsibilities. (Bill Maher)

If our Founding Fathers wanted us to care about the rest of the world, they wouldn't have declared their independence from it. (Stephen Colbert)

It's amazing that the amount of news that happens in the world everyday always just exactly fits the newspaper, (Jerry Seinfeld)

The best argument against democracy is a five-minute conversation with the average voter. (Winston Churchill)

Half of the American people have never read a newspaper. Half never voted for President. One hopes it is the same half. (Gore Vidal)

In revolutions there are only two sorts of men, those who cause them and those who profit by them. (Napoleon)

The future is already here; it's just unevenly distributed. (William Gibson)

I sit on a man's back, choking him and making him carry me, and yet assure myself and others that I am very sorry for him and wish to ease his lot by all possible means...except by getting off his back. (Leo Tolstoy)

Socialism never took root in America because the poor see themselves not as exploited proletariat but as temporarily embarrassed millionaires. (John Steinbeck)

My job is to inspire people to take ownership of this country. Politics is not a business. It's a mission. It's about making people's lives better. (Barack Obama)

The design of political language: To make lies sound truthful and murder respectable, and to give an appearance of solidity to pure wind. (George Orwell)

One of the best ways to get yourself a reputation as a dangerous citizen these days is to go about repeating the very phrases which our Founding Fathers used in the struggle for independence. (Charles Austin Beard)

This country's got the best politicians money can buy. (Will Rogers)

The United States is a nation of laws: badly written and randomly enforced. (Frank Zappa)

A jury consists of twelve persons chosen to decide who has the better lawyer. (Robert Frost)

Justice ought to be fair. (George W. Bush)

A doubtful friend is worse than a certain enemy. Let a man be one thing or the other, and then we know how to meet him. (Aesop)

If God had wanted us to vote, he'd have given us candidates. (Jay Leno)

In war, truth is the first casualty. (Aeschylus)

I learned to slip back and forth between my black and white worlds. One of the tricks I learned: People were satisfied so long as you were courteous and smiled and made no sudden moves. They were more than satisfied; they were relieved--such a pleasant surprise to find a well-mannered young black man who didn't seem angry all the time. (Barack Obama)

They say, "Guns don't kill people, people kill people." But I think the guns help. Just standing there saying, "Bang!" doesn't really hurt anybody. (Eddie Izzard)

The fox condemns the trap, not himself. (William Blake)

It is dangerous to be right when the government is wrong. (Voltaire)

In the United States, anybody can be president. That's the problem. (George Carlin)

When we're talking about war, we're really talking about peace. (George W. Bush)

There's no trick when it comes to being a humorist when you have the whole government working for you. (Will Rogers)

Common sense is not so common. (Voltaire)

The earth has enough for every man's need, but not for every man's greed. (Mahatma Gandhi)

There is inherited wealth in this country and also inherited poverty. (John F. Kennedy)

I don't make jokes. I just watch the government and report the facts. (Will Rogers)

Jesse Ventura on gun control: "My definition is standing at 25 meters and putting two rounds in the same hole. That's gun control."

Religion is what keeps the poor from murdering the rich. (Napoleon Bonaparte)

Fix the problem, not the blame. (Japanese saying, "Rising Sun," Michael Crichton)

Business is war. (Japanese motto, "Rising Sun", Michael Crichton)

I believe in the all-seeing eye watching us from above. Unfortunately, this eye is the government. (Woody Allen)

Politics is show business for ugly people. (Paul Begala)

A problem well stated is a problem half solved. (Charles F. Kettering, inventor)

The reason there are two senators from each state is so one can be the designated driver. (Jay Leno)

Just because you do not take an interest in politics doesn't mean politics won't take an interest in you. (Pericles-430 B.C.)

The end move in politics is always to pick up a gun. (R. Buckminster Fuller)

There never was a good war or a bad peace. (Benjamin Franklin)

If you can't stand the heat stay out of the kitchen. (Harry Truman)

If hypocrisy was gold, the Capitol would be Fort Knox. (Senator John McCain)

Maybe if we did a better job of listening, history wouldn't have to repeat itself.

There are no warlike peoples, just warlike leaders. (Ralph Bunche)

The one thing that unites all human beings, regardless of age, gender, religion, economic status or ethnic background, is that deep down inside, we all believe that we are above average drivers. (Dave Barry)

Those of you that will give up your liberty for security shall have and deserve neither. Liberty is security. (Ben Franklin)

Sometimes I think war is God's way of teaching us geography. (Paul Rodriguez)

The penalty that good men pay for not being interested in politics is to be governed by men worse than themselves. (Plato)

Politics is not a bad profession. If you succeed there are many rewards, if you disgrace yourself you can always write a book. (Ronald Reagan)

When elephants fight, it's the grass that suffers. (African Proverb)

In war, there are no unwounded soldiers. (Jose Narosky)

Nationalism is an infantile disease. It is the measles of mankind. (Albert Einstein)

Bureaucracy is the art of making the possible impossible. (Javier Pascual Salcedo)

A camel is what you get when you form a committee to design a horse.

The idea that you can merchandise candidates for high office like breakfast cereal is the ultimate indignity to the democratic process. (Adlai E. Stevenson)

Whenever you find yourself on the side of the majority, it is time to pause and reflect. (Mark Twain)

A great many people in this country are worried about law and order. And a great many people are worried about justice. But one thing is certain: you cannot have either until you have both. (Ramsey Clark)

Freedom is the oxygen of the soul. (Moshe Dayan)

The clash of ideas is the sound of freedom. (Graffiti)

Those who profess to favor freedom and yet depreciate agitation are men who want rain without thunder and lightning. (Frederick Douglass)

Just because everything is different doesn't mean anything has changed. (Irene Peter)

You can't ride two horses with one butt.

Man plans. God laughs. (Yiddish proverb)

Reader, suppose you were an idiot. And suppose you were a member of Congress. But I repeat myself. (Mark Twain)

If you want to rise, lift up the people around you.

Anyone who has ever struggled with poverty knows how extremely expensive it is to be poor. (James Baldwin)

George Washington's brother, Lawrence, was the Uncle

of Our Country. (George Carlin)

Remember, remember always that all of us, and you and I especially, are descended from immigrants and revolutionists. (Franklin D. Roosevelt)

I'd kill for the Nobel Peace Prize. (Steven Wright)

The love of one's country is a splendid thing. But why should love stop at the border. (Pablo Casals)

Those who can make you believe absurdities can make you commit atrocities. (Voltaire)

Someday they'll announce a war and nobody will come. (Carl Sandburg)

If an elephant has its foot on the tail of a mouse and you say that you are neutral, the mouse will not appreciate your neutrality. (Bishop Desmond Tutu)

There's not a liberal America and a conservative America; there's the United States of America. There's not a black America and white America and Latino America and Asian America; there's the United States of America. (Barack Obama, 2004)

The nice thing about being a celebrity is that, if you bore people, they think it's their fault. (Henry Kissinger)

I just don't know why they're shooting at us. All we want to do is bring them democracy and white bread. Transplant the American Dream. Freedom. Achievement. Hyperacidity. Affluence. Flatulence. Technology. Tension. The inalienable right to an early coronary sitting at your desk while plotting to stab your boss in the back. (Alan Alda as Hawkeye in M*A*S*H)

History is written by the winners. (George Orwell)

I have a scheme for stopping war. It's this: no nation is allowed to enter a war until they have paid for the last one. (Will Rogers)

The best leader is the one who, after it happens, the people think they did it themselves. (Lao Tzu)

The more you observe politics, the more you've got to admit that each party is worse than the other. (Will Rogers)

Man is a Religious Animal. He is the only Religious Animal. He is the only animal that has the True Religion—several of them. He is the only animal that loves his neighbor as himself and cuts his throat if his theology isn't straight. He has made a graveyard of the globe in trying his honest best to smooth his brother's path to happiness and heaven. (Mark Twain)

If you believe everything you read, better not read. (Japanese proverb)

Another plan I have is World Peace through Formal Introductions. The idea is that everyone in the world would be required to meet everyone else in the world, formally, at least once. You'd have to look the person in the eye, shake hands, repeat their name, and try to remember one outstanding physical characteristic. My theory is, if you knew everyone in the world personally, you'd be less inclined to fight them in a war: "Who? The Malaysians? Are you kidding? I know those people!" (George Carlin)

Ohio claims they are due a president as they haven't had one since Taft. Look at the United States. They have not had one since Lincoln. (Will Rogers)

This problem with illegal immigration is nothing new. In fact, the Indians had a special name for it. They called it "white people." (Jay Leno)

God is love, but get it in writing. (Gypsy Rose Lee)

You've got to have something to eat and a little love in your life before you can hold still for any damn body's sermon on how to behave. (Billie Holiday)

Ideologies separate us. Dreams and anguish bring us together. (Eugene Ionesco)

The world is divided into haves and have-nots: those who have a sense of humor and those who do not. (Jason Love)

Too often we enjoy the comfort of opinion without the discomfort of thought. (John F. Kennedy)

Progress is a nice word. But change is its motivator. And change has its enemies. (Robert F. Kennedy)

A kindergarten teacher was showing her class an encyclopedia page picturing several national flags. She pointed to the American flag and asked, "What flag is this?"
A little girl called out, "That's the flag of our country."
"Very good," the teacher said. "And what is the name of our country?"
"'Tis of thee," the girl said confidently.

Benjamin Franklin gave guitar lessons.

Only law can give us freedom. (Goethe)

George Washington's feet were a size 13.

144

Washing one's hands of the conflict between the powerful and the powerless means to side with the powerful. (Paulo Freire)

You can fool all the people all the time if the advertising is right and the budget is big enough. (Joseph E. Levine)

You know you can never find out what's happening from the company bulletin or the adult press. You know that. The king's messengers are always telling you what they want you to know, for their own benefit. The evolutionary message, what's really happening, has always come from outcasts. (Timothy Leary)

I think it would be a good idea. (Mahatma Ghandi, when asked what he thought of Western Civilization)

We learn from history that we do not learn from history. (Hegel)

Under Republicans, man exploits man. Under Democrats, it's just the opposite.

History teaches us the mistakes we are going to make. (Laurence J. Peter)

A Brief History of Our Times: As television became flatter, people became rounder. (Aaron Caro's Ruminations.com)

There is a cult of ignorance in the United States, and there always has been...nurtured by the false notion that democracy means that "my ignorance is just as good as your knowledge." (Isaac Asimov)

In this country "America" means white. Everybody else has to hyphenate. (Toni Morrison)

The conquest of the earth, which mostly means the taking away from those who have a different complexion or slightly flatter noses than ourselves, is not a pretty thing when you look into it. (Joseph Conrad)

Sometimes I feel discriminated against, but it does not make my angry. It merely astonishes me. How can any deny themselves the pleasure of my company? (Zora Neal Hurston)

The best politics is right action. (Mahatma Gandhi)

History is a nightmare from which we are trying to awaken. (James Joyce)

Washington is a city of southern efficiency and northern charm. (John F. Kennedy)

Too bad 90% of the politicians give the other 10% a bad reputation. (Henry Kissinger)

Sticks in a bundle are unbreakable. (African Proverb)

When fire and water are at war, it is the fire that loses. (Spanish proverb)

They call it the "American Dream" because you have to be asleep to believe it. (George Carlin)

What are the seven deadly sins of Christianity? Gluttony, avarice, sloth, lust…They are urges every man feels at least once a day. How could you set yourself up as the most powerful institution on earth? You first find out what every man feels at least once a day, establish that as a sin, and set yourself up as the only institution capable of pardoning that sin. (Anton LaVey)

The man who strikes first admits that his ideas have given out. (Chinese proverb)

Always be sincere, even if you don't mean it. (Harry Truman)

The law, in its majestic equality, forbids the rich as well as the poor to sleep under bridges, to beg in the streets, and to steal bread. (Anatole France)

The human race has improved everything but the human race. (Adlai Stevenson)

I have decided to stick with love. Hate is too great a burden to bear. (Martin Luther King, Jr.)

The guns and the bombs, the rockets and the warships, are all symbols of human failure. (Lyndon B. Johnson)

The only real struggle in the history of the world is between the vested interest and social justice. (Arnold Toynbee)

The Bible is an oral history. It was passed down, word of mouth, father to son, from Adam to Seth, from Seth to Enos, from Enos to Cainan, for forty generations, a growing, changing story...until Moses finally gets it down on lambskin. But lambskins wear out, and need to be recopied. Copies of copies of copies of copies of copies of copies of copies of an oral history passed down through forty generations. From Hebrew it's translated into Arabic, from Arabic to Latin, from Latin to Greek, from Greek to Russian, from Russian to German, from German to an old form of English that you could not read...You can't put a grocery list through that many translations, copies, and retellings, and not expect to have some big changes in the dinner menu when the kids make it back from Kroger. And yet people are killing each other over this written word. Here's a tip: if you're killing someone in the name of God, you are missing the message. (Nick Annis)

Conservatives define themselves in terms of what they oppose. (George Will)

Man becomes great exactly in the degree to which he works for the welfare of his fellow men. (Mahatma Gandhi)

America is the only country that went from barbarism to decadence without civilization in between. (Oscar Wilde)

There's a stereotype that black people are lazy. I don't know if that's true, but I know white people went all the way to Africa to get out of doing work. (Lance Crouther)

I destroy my enemy by making him my friend. (Abraham Lincoln)

Politics is the shadow cast over society by big business. (John Dewey)

One of the things Jesus did was to step aside from the organized religion of his time because it had become corrupt and bogged down with rules. Rules became more important than feeding the hungry. (Corita Kent)

War will exist until that distant day when the conscientious objector enjoys the same reputation and prestige that the warrior does today. (John F. Kennedy)

An honest man in politics shines more than he would elsewhere. (Mark Twain)

I don't believe there's any problem in this country, no matter how tough it is, that Americans, when they roll up their sleeves, can't completely ignore. (George Carlin)

His inventions created millions of new jobs. Edison has done more toward abolishing poverty than all the reformers and statesmen. (Henry Ford)

It does me no injury for my neighbor to say there are twenty gods or no gods. (Thomas Jefferson)

The best way to predict the future is to invent it. (Alan Kay, computer scientist)

What this country needs is more out-of-work politicians. (Angela Davis)

It's not that ordinary people have forgotten how to dream. It's just that their leaders have forgotten how. (Barack Obama)

We are called the nation of inventors. And we are. We could still claim that title and wear its loftiest honors if we had stopped with the first thing we had ever invented— human liberty. (Mark Twain)

Washington is "Mr. Smith Goes to Washington" without the happy ending. (Howard Ogden)

QUESTIONS

If corn oil comes from corn, and olive oil comes from olives...where does baby oil come from?

What if Aretha Franklin married Buddy Holly? She'd be Aretha Holly.

Who needs rhetorical questions?

If "Quitters never win and winners never quit," who came up with "Quit while you're ahead?"

If athletes get athlete's foot, do astronauts get mistletoe?

Why is "phonics" not spelled the way it sounds?

Can a hearse carrying a corpse drive in the carpool lane?

If truth is beauty, how come no one has her hair done in a library? (Lily Tomlin)

Why do they put up pictures of criminals in the post office? What are we supposed to do...write to them?

Why are you *IN* a movie, but you're *ON* TV?

When blondes have more fun...do they know it?

If Man evolved from the monkeys and apes...why do we still have monkeys and apes?

What washes up on really small beaches?...Microwaves.

If you wear an antenna to your wedding...do you get better reception?

Why don't cannibals eat clowns? They taste funny.

Why is a man who invests all your money called a broker?

What do you have when a midget fortune-teller escapes from prison? A small medium at large.

Why do they lock gas station bathrooms? Are they afraid someone will clean them?

If "Love is blind"…why is lingerie so popular?

If a pig loses its voice…is it disgruntled?

If you try to fail and you succeed, what did you just do?

What's another word for "Thesaurus?" (Steven Wright)

If "All the world is a stage"…where is the audience sitting?

Why do we sing "Take Me Out To The Ball Game" when we are already there?

If "Ignorance is bliss," why aren't more people happy?

What happens if you get scared half to death, twice?

What is a "free" gift? Aren't all gifts free?

Did Adam and Eve have navels?

Why are there interstate highways in Hawaii?

If you shoot at a mime, should you use a silencer? (Steven Wright)

Why is the third hand on a watch called the second hand?

Can you be a closet claustrophobic?

Why don't they have dessert at breakfast?

If I live in a fantasy world, why do I have to pay taxes? (Rita Rudner)

What is the difference between a slim chance and a fat chance?

If one synchronized swimmer drowns, do the rest drown too?

When someone offers you a penny for your thoughts, and you put in your two cents worth, what happens to the other penny?

What if there were no hypothetical questions?

If a deaf person has to go to court, is it still called a hearing?

If a turtle doesn't have a shell, is he homeless or naked?

RIMSHOT DANDIES

How much do pirates pay for their earrings?...A buccaneer.

Why do seagulls fly over the sea?...Because if they flew over the bay, they'd be bagels.

A man was driving around the block in a sweat because he had an important meeting and couldn't find a parking place. Around and around he drove, but no one was pulling out. Looking up toward heaven, he said "Lord, take pity on me. If you find me a parking place I will go to church every Sunday for the rest of my life and give up drinking!" Miraculously, a parking place appeared. As the man pulled into the space, he looked up to heaven once more and said..."Never mind. I found one."

Why don't mummies take vacations?...They are afraid they will relax and unwind.

Two Eskimos sitting in a kayak were chilly, so they lit a fire in the craft. Unsurprisingly it sank, proving once again that you can't have your kayak and heat it too.

I used to work at a fire hydrant factory. You couldn't park anywhere near the place. (Steven Wright)

Mahatma Gandhi, as you know, walked barefoot most of the time, which produced an impressive set of calluses on his feet. He also ate very little, which made him rather frail and, with his odd diet, he suffered from bad breath. This made him a super calloused fragile mystic hexed by halitosis.

Why did the chicken go to the séance?...To get to the other side.

What kind of clothes do lawyers wear?...Lawsuits.

Hopelessly lost, the man pulled his car into an abandoned gas station in the desert and got out. The only creature there was an owl sitting on a cactus. "Owl, are you able to tell me the quickest way to town?"
"Are you walking or driving?" asked the wise owl.
"I'm driving."
"Well, that's the quickest way."

How many people with no sense of humor does it take to change a lightbulb?...One.

What do you call a deer with no eyes?...No idea.

Sherlock Holmes and Dr. Watson went on a camping trip. After a good meal and a bottle of wine, they lay down in their tent for the night and went to sleep. Some hours later, Holmes awoke and nudged his faithful friend.
"Watson...look up at the sky and tell me what you see."
Watson replied: "I see a million stars."
"What does that tell you?" Holmes questioned.
Watson pondered for a minute...then replied:
"Astronomically, it tells me that there are millions of galaxies and potentially billions of planets. Astrologically, I observe that Saturn is in Leo. Horologically, I deduce that the time is approximately a quarter past three. Theologically, I can see that God is all-powerful and that we are small and insignificant. Meteorologically, I suspect that we will have a beautiful day tomorrow. What does it tell you?" Watson asked.
Holmes was silent for a moment...and then spoke:
"Watson, you twit!...Someone has stolen our tent!"

Dying man: You know, honey, you've always been with me through all my troubles. Through all my bad times,

you've been there. When I got fired, you were there. When my business went down the toilet, you were there. When I had the heart attack, you were there. You know something?
Woman: What?
Dying man: I think you're bad luck

Did you hear about the guy whose whole left side was cut off?...He's all right now.

There was a magician working on a cruise ship. He had a parrot that was always ruining his act, saying in the middle of a trick, "The card is up his sleeve," or "He has a dove in his pocket," or "He slipped it through a hole in his hat." One day the ship sank. The parrot and the magician found themselves together on a life raft. For several days, the parrot sat silent and stared at the magician. On the fourth day, the parrot said, "Okay, I give up. What did you do with the ship?"

Jill, a blonde, approaches the edge of a river. On the other side she sees another blonde. Jill asks her, "How do I get to the other side of the river?" The blonde responds, "You're already on the other side."

A man walks into a cardiologist's office...
Man: "Excuse me. Can you help me? I think I'm a moth."
Doctor: "You don't need a cardiologist. You need a psychiatrist."
Man: "Yes, I know."
Doctor: "So why did you come in here if you need a psychiatrist?"
Man: "Well, the light was on..."

Knock, knock.
Who's there?
Duane

Duane who?
Duane the bathtub, I'm dwowning!

Build a man a fire and he'll be warm for a day. Set a man on fire and he'll be warm for the rest of his life.

Two guys are out walking their dogs. One has a German Shepard and one has a Chihuahua. It's a summer day and it's very hot.
Mr. Chihuahua: "Man, it is HOT! I could sure stand a cold beer."
Mr. Shepard: "I know what you mean. Hey, I know a place. Just follow me."
They walk a couple blocks and get to a bar and with a big sign outside announcing…"NO DOGS ALLOWED."
Mr. Chihuahua: "Look at that sign! We can't go in there with these dogs."
Mr. Shepard: "I've done this before. Listen. I'll go in first. Just watch me and do what I do and there's no problem."
So the guy with the Chihuahua stands at the door and the guy with the German Shepard goes inside and sits down on a bar stool, the dog sitting on the floor next to him. The bartender comes over.
Bartender: " 'Afternoon, buddy. What can I do for you?"
Guy: "I'd like a cold beer."
Bartender: "I'm sorry, but I can't serve you with the dog in here."
Guy: "It's a seeing-eye dog."
Bartender: "Well…okay then."
And he serves him a beer. The guy with the Chihuahua walks in, sits down on a bar stool. The Chihuahua sits on the floor next to him. The bartender comes over.
Bartender: "'Afternoon, buddy. What can I do for you?"
Guy: "I'd like a cold beer."
Bartender: "I'm sorry, but I can't serve you with the dog in here."
Guy: "It's a seeing-eye dog."

The bartender leans over the bar to take a closer look at the dog.
Bartender: "But it's a Chihuahua!"
Guy: "You mean, they gave me a Chihuahua?!!" (Bob Devine)

A man asks his dentist, "Do you have anything for yellow teeth?" The dentist replies, "How about a brown tie?"

A widow goes to a psychic to try to communicate with her dead husband. The psychic tells her there are three options, $25, $50 & $100.
"For $25, I will contact your husband and you can speak to him. For $50, I will contact your husband, you can speak to him and he will answer you."
"What will I get for $100?"
"For $100, I will contact your husband, you can speak to him and he will answer you while I drink a glass of water."

Knock, knock.
Who's there?
Control freak. Now you say, "control freak who?"

One ship carrying blue paint collided with another ship carrying red paint. The crew is missing and believed to be marooned.

Did you hear about the agnostic, dyslexic insomniac? He stayed up all night wondering if there was a Dog.

Nurse (to Doctor): The Invisible Man is in the waiting room.
Doctor: Tell him I can't see him right now.

I told my doctor I broke my leg in two places. He told me to quit going to those places. (Henny Youngman)

Yesterday I told a chicken to cross the road. It said, "What for?"

A three-legged dog walks into a saloon in the Old West. He sidles up to the bar and announces: "I'm looking for the man who shot my paw."

Did you hear about the man who fell into the upholstery machine? He's completely recovered.

What has 200 legs and 5 teeth?…the front row at a Willie Nelson concert.

I don't care what anybody says about me as long as it isn't true. (Truman Capote)

My neighbor has a circular driveway. He can't get out. (Steven Wright)

A dyslexic man walks into a bra.

What do you call a dog with no legs?…It doesn't matter what you call him, he ain't comin. (Dom Irera)

Two eggs, a bagel and a sausage walk into a bar. "Bartender, my friends and I would like a cold one," says one of the eggs. "Sorry," the barman replies. "We don't serve breakfast."

Patient: Doctor, you told me I have a month to live and then you sent me a bill for $1,000! I can't pay that before the end of the month!
Doctor: Okay, you have six months to live.

This guy goes into his barber, and he's all excited. He says, "I'm going to go to Rome. I'm flying on Alitalia and staying at the Rome Hilton, and I'm going to see the

Pope." The barber says, "Ha! Alitalia is a terrible airline, the Rome Hilton is a dump, and when you see the Pope, you'll probably be standing in back of about 10,000 people."

So the guy goes to Rome and comes back. His barber asks, "How was it?"

"Great," he says. "Alitalia was a wonderful airline. The hotel was great. And I got to meet the Pope."

"You met the Pope?" said the barber.

"I bent down to kiss the Pope's ring."

"And what did he say?"

"He said, 'Where did you get that crummy haircut?"

I fired my masseuse today...she rubbed me the wrong way.

Did you hear about the dyslexic devil worshipper?...He sold his soul to Santa.

At a convention of blondes, a speaker insisted that the "dumb blonde" myth is all wrong. To prove it he asked one young volunteer, "How much is 101 plus 20?"

The blonde answered, "120."

"No," he said, "that's not right."

The audience called out, "Give her another chance."

So the speaker asked the blonde, "How much is 10 plus 13?"

Slowly the blonde replied, "16."

"Sorry," he said, shaking his head.

"Give her another chance," the audience called out again.

The speaker responded slowly, "Okay then, how much is 2 plus 2?"

The blonde sheepishly replied, "Four?"

The audience called out, "Give her another chance!"

People who jump off a Paris bridge are in Seine.

What a hotel! The towels were so fluffy I could hardly close my suitcase. (Henny Youngman)

Two guys are walking through the woods and come across this big deep hole.
"Wow...that looks deep."
"Sure does... toss a few pebbles in there and see how deep it is."
They pick up a few pebbles and throw them in and wait... no noise.
"Jeeez. That is REALLY deep... here... throw one of these great big rocks down there. Those should make a noise."
They pick up a couple football-sized rocks and toss them into the hole and wait... and wait. Nothing. They look at each other in amazement. One gets a determined look on his face and says, "Hey...over here in the weeds, there's a railroad tie. Help me carry it over here. When we toss THAT sucker in, it's GOTTA make some noise."
The two drag the heavy tie over to the hole and heave it in. Not a sound comes from the hole. Suddenly, out of the nearby woods, a goat appears, running like the wind. It rushes toward the two men, then right past them, running as fast as it's legs will carry it. Suddenly it leaps in the air and into the hole. The two men are astonished with what they've just seen...Then, out of the woods comes a farmer who spots the men and ambles over.
"Hey... you two guys seen my goat out here?"
"You bet we did! Craziest thing I ever seen. It came running like crazy and just jumped into this hole!"
"Nah", says the farmer, "That couldn't have been MY goat. My goat was chained to a railroad tie."

I went to a seafood disco last week...and pulled a mussel.

What's the difference between a circus clown and a Roman barber? One's a raving showman and other's a shaving Roman. (Paul Wagner)

A Pollack, a lawyer and a blond walk into a bar. The barman leans over the bar and says, "Hey, what is this?...A joke?!"

Oh! Oh! Oh!...Dyslexic Santa.

Two gypsy fortune-tellers meet on the street: "You're fine. How am I?"

What do you call a Mexican with a rubber toe?...Roberto.

How do you know the toothbrush was invented in Tennessee?...If it had been invented anywhere else it would have been called the teethbrush. (David Jackson)

E-mail from God:
One day God was looking down at Earth and saw all of the evil that was going on. He decided to send an angel to check it out. He called on a female angel and sent her to Earth for a short time. When she returned she told God, "Yes, it is bad on Earth - 95% is bad and 5% is good." God thought for a moment and said, "Maybe I had better send a male angel--to get both points of view." When the male angel returned he told God, "Yes, the Earth is in serious decline--95% bad and 5% good." God knew this was quite serious. He decided to e-mail the 5% that were good, to encourage them, to provide that little something to help them keep going. Do you know what that e-mail said? You mean you didn't get one either???!!!

SCHOOL

I began my education at a very early age...in fact, right after I left college. (Winston Churchill)

I have never let my schooling interfere with my education. (Mark Twain)

A psychology professor and a history professor are sitting on the porch of a nudist colony watching the sunset. The historian says to the psychologist, "Have you read Marx?" The psychology professor replies, "Yes. I think it's the wicker chairs."

People only see what they are prepared to see. (Ralph Waldo Emerson)

In real life, I assure you, there is no such thing as algebra. (Fran Lebowitz)

You have to be an intellectual to believe such nonsense. No ordinary man could be such a fool. (George Orwell)

A great many people think they are thinking when they are merely rearranging their prejudices. (William James)

It is a miracle that curiosity survives formal education. (Albert Einstein)

Everything we really need to know we learned in kindergarten (Robert Fulghum)

Good teaching is one-fourth preparation and three-fourths theater. (Gail Goodwin)

It is the mark of an educated mind to be able to entertain a thought without accepting it. (Aristotle)

TCHR(heart)3R (License plate)

You know there is a problem with the education system when you realize that out of the three Rs, only one begins with an R. (Dennis Miller)

He who opens a school door, closes a prison. (Victor Hugo)

A child educated only at school is an uneducated child. (Georges Santayana)

Example isn`t another way to teach, it is the only way to teach. (Albert Einstein)

Think before you speak. Read before you think. (Fran Lebowitz)

You're never too old to learn something stupid.

I cannot teach anybody anything; I can only make them think. (Socrates)

How is it that little children are so intelligent and men so stupid? It must be education that does it. (Alexandre Dumas)

By not going to school I learned that the world is a beautiful place and needs to be discovered. (Rutger Hauer)

Education is not the learning of facts, but the training of the mind to think. (Albert Einstein)

In some parts of the world, students are going to school every day. It's their normal life. But in other part of the world, we are starving for education... it's like a precious gift. It's like a diamond. (Malala Yousafzai)

I went to a public school through sixth grade, and being good at tests wasn't cool. (Bill Gates)

It is important that students bring a certain ragamuffin, barefoot irreverence to their studies; they are not here to worship what is known but question it. (Jacob Bronowski)

We don't stop going to school when we graduate. (Carol Burnett)

Sixty years ago I knew everything; now I know nothing; education is a progressive discovery of our own ignorance. (Will Durant)

I went to a boys' school, and I didn't realize that most guys join bands because they wanted to get girls. I was not really focused on that the way everybody else was. (Thom Yorke)

If I ran a school, I'd give the average grade to the ones who gave me all the right answers, for being good little parrots. I'd give the top grades to those who made a lot of mistakes and told me about them, and then told me what they learned from them. (R. Buckminster Fuller)

They used to complain at school that I looked out of the window for long periods of time. That sums up my life. I like to look out the window, do nothing, daydream. (Ritchie Blackmore)

Education is what remains after one has forgotten what one has learned in school. (Albert Einstein)

A young lad was sent to school. He began his lessons with the other children, and the first lesson the teacher taught him was the straight line, the figure "one." But whereas the others went on progressing, this child continued to write the same figure. After two or three days the teacher came up to him and said, "Have you finished your lesson?" He said, "No, I'm still writing 'one.'" He went on doing the same thing, and when at the end of the week the teacher asked him again he said, "I have not finished it." The teacher thought he was an idiot and should be sent away, as he could or did not want to learn. At home the child continued with the same exercise and the parents also became tired and disgusted. He simply said, "I have not yet learned it, I am learning it. When I have finished I shall take the other lessons." The parents said, "The other children are going on further, school has given you up, and you do not show any progress; we are tired of you." And the lad thought with a sad heart that as he had displeased his parents, too, he had better leave home. So he went into the wilderness and lived on fruits and nuts. After a long time he returned to his old school. And when he saw the teacher he said to him, "I think I have learned it. See if I have. Shall I write on this wall?" And when he made his sign the wall split in two. (Hazrat Inayat Khan)

You can lead a fool to knowledge but you can't make him think.

I have come to believe that a great teacher is a great artist and that there are as few as there are any other great artists. Teaching might even be the greatest of the arts since the medium is the human mind and spirit. (John Steinbeck)

SCIENCE & TECHNOLOGY

We could hardly wait to get up in the morning. (Wilbur and Orville Wright-Inventors of the airplane)

1 millionth of a mouthwash = 1 microscope
Time between slipping on a peel and smacking the pavement = 1 bananosecond
Weight an evangelist carries with God = 1 billigram
Time it takes to sail 220 yards at 1 nautical mile per hour = Knotfurlong
16.5 feet in the Twilight Zone = 1 Rod Sterling
Half of a large intestine = 1 semicolon
1,000,000 aches = 1 megahurtz
Basic unit of laryngitis = 1 hoarsepower
Shortest distance between two jokes = A straight line
453.6 graham crackers = 1 pound cake
1 million-million microphones = 1 megaphone
2 million bicycles = 2 megacycles
365.25 days = 1 unicycle
2000 mockingbirds = 2 kilomockingbirds
52 cards = 1 decacards
Ratio of an igloo's circumference to its diameter = Eskimo Pi

I have not failed. I've just found 10,000 ways that don't work. (Thomas Edison)

In my opinion, we don't devote nearly enough scientific research to finding a cure for jerks. (Bill Watterson, "Calvin & Hobbs")

MARSN8V (License plate)

The computer, the noise of the computer, feels like impatience. It's sort of the sound of impatience to me. (Tony Kushner)

Science is not only compatible with spirituality; it is a profound source of spirituality. (Carl Sagan)

I don't care that they stole my idea; I care that they don't have any of their own. (Nikola Tesla)

Progress is man's ability to complicate simplicity. (Thor Heyerdahl)

Kilometers are shorter than miles. Save gas; take your next trip in kilometers. (George Carlin)

It has become appallingly obvious that our technology has exceeded our humanity. (Albert Einstein)

Yesterday I got my tie caught in a fax machine. Next thing I knew, I was in Los Angeles. (Steve Haupt)

My password is MickeyMinnieGoofyPluto, because it has to be at least four characters.

When chemists die, they barium. (Punography)

Computers aren't intelligent, they only think they are. (Emo Philips)

All toasters should be see-through. (Aaron Karo-Ruminations.com)

Progress might have been all right once, but it has gone on too long. (Ogden Nash)

We breathe oxygen by day; by night, we breathe nitrogen.

In my school, the brightest boys did math and physics,

the less bright did physics and chemistry, and the least bright did biology. I wanted to do math and physics, but my father made me do chemistry because he thought there would be no jobs for mathematicians. (Stephan Hawking)

Science does not know it's debt to imagination. (Ralph Waldo Emerson)

If television's a babysitter, the Internet is a drunk librarian who won't shut up. (Dorothy Gambrell)

Do radioactive cats have eighteen half-lives? (Steven Wright)

I always give my future-self way too much credit when it comes to remembering passwords. (Aaron Karo's Ruminations.com)

The most likely way for the world to be destroyed, most experts say, is by accident. That's where we come in; we're computer professionals. We cause accidents. (Nathaniel Borenstein)

We've all heard that a million monkeys banging on a million typewriters will eventually reproduce the entire works of Shakespeare. Now, thanks to the Internet, we know this is not true. (Robert Wilensky)

Television is an invention that permits you to be entertained in your living room by people you wouldn't have in your home. (David Frost)

I think computer viruses should count as life. I think it says something about human nature that the only form of life we have created so far is purely destructive.

We've created life in our own image. (Stephen Hawking)

It's a small world, but I wouldn't want to have to paint it. (Steven Wright)

For a list of all the ways technology has failed to improve the quality of life, please press 3. (Alice Kahn)

Why do toasters always have a setting that burns toast to a horrible crisp, which no decent human being would eat?

I don't want a smart phone; I want a wise phone. (Sparrow)

If it keeps up, man will atrophy all his limbs but the push-button finger. (Frank Lloyd Wright)

Who invented the first plane that wouldn't fly?...The Wrong Brothers. (Sean)

There is geometry in the ringing of strings. There is harmony in the spacing of the spheres. (Pythagoras)

I think God's going to come down and pull civilization over for speeding. (Steven Wright)

I have always wished that my computer would be as easy to use as my telephone. My wish has come true. I no longer know how to use my telephone. (Bjarne Stroustrup)

I changed my iPod's name to "Titanic." It's syncing now. (M. D. Rosenberg)

I replaced the headlights on my car with strobe lights. Now it looks like I'm the only one moving. (Steven Wright)

Don't fight forces; use them. (R. Buckminster Fuller)

Men travel faster now, but I do not know if they go to better things. (Willa Cather)

Using my phone, I took a picture of my camera. (Sparrow)

As an adolescent I aspired to lasting fame, I craved factual certainty, and I thirsted for a meaningful vision of human life…so I became a scientist. This is like becoming an archbishop so you can meet girls. (Matt Cartmill)

Don't worry about the world coming to an end today. It's already tomorrow in Australia. (Charles Schulz)

Leonardo Da Vinci invented the scissors.

I just bought a microwave fireplace. You can spend an entire evening in front of it in only eight minutes. (Steven Wright)

In science it often happens that scientists say, "You know, that's a really good argument; my position is mistaken," and then they actually change their minds, and you never hear that old view from them again. They really do it. It doesn't happen as often as it should, because scientists are human and change is sometimes painful. But it happens every day. I cannot recall the last time that something like that happened in politics or religion. (Carl Sagan)

Artificial Intelligence is no match for natural stupidity.

Yawning is your body's way of saying '20 per cent battery remaining'.

The first e-mail was sent over the internet in 1972.

A hen is only an egg's way of making another egg.

Before electric lighting, did we have acoustic lighting? (Joe Futrelle)

When you sit with a nice girl for two hours you think it's only a minute. But when you sit on a hot stove for a minute you think it's two hours. That's relativity. (Albert Einstein)

The only proof that there is intelligent life on other planets is that they haven't landed on earth. (Calvin & Hobbs)

Never let a computer know you're in a hurry.

Computers are useless. They can only give you answers. (Pablo Picasso)

I bought the latest computer
    It came completely loaded
It was guaranteed for 90 days
    but in 30 was outmoded

Time is Nature's way of preventing everything from happening at once.

What three things make up an atom? Neutrons, protons and croutons. (Ben, 8, Edgemont Elementary)

Every time I ask what time it is, I get a different answer. (Henny Youngman)

Sign on an electrician's truck: "Let us remove your shorts."

We may prefer to think of ourselves as fallen angels, but in reality we are risen apes. (Desmond Morris)

Scientists at the California Institute of Technology's "Infrared Processing and Analysis Center" study data from outer space transmitted by our satellites. They also relax and get exercise by playing on a softball team. The name of their team?...The Infrared Sox.

New restaurant on the moon...great food...great prices...no atmosphere.

186,000 miles per second...Not just a good idea...It's the law!!

Life is extinct on other planets because their scientists were more advanced than ours.

If you're in a vehicle going the speed of light, what happens when you turn on the headlights?

If you can't fix it with duct tape, it's broken. (Mike Malone)

H_2O is hot water, and CO_2 is cold water.

Water is composed of two gins, Oxygin and Hydrogin. Oxygin is pure gin. Hydrogin is gin and water.

One of television's great contributions is that it brought murder back into the home, where it belongs. (Alfred Hitchcock)

A fossil is an extinct animal. The older it is, the more extinct it is.

Okay, so what's the speed of dark?

The difference between stupidity and genius is that genius has its limits. (Albert Einstein)

The system of nature, of which man is a part, tends to be self-balancing, self-adjusting, self-cleansing. Not so with technology. (E.F. Schumacher)

I think the outcome would be much as when Christopher Columbus first landed in America, which didn't turn out very well for the Native Americans. (Stephen Hawking, British physicist, hypothesizing the consequences of aliens visiting Earth)

Light travels faster than sound. That's why some people appear bright until you hear them speak.

Star Wars: A long time ago, but somehow still in the future.

To the optimist, the glass is half-full. To the pessimist, the glass is half empty. To the engineer, the glass is twice as big as it needs to be.

If electricity comes from electrons, does morality come from morons?

The sun, with all those planets revolving around it and dependent on it, can still ripen a bunch of grapes as if it had nothing else in the universe to do. (Galileo)

It doesn't matter what temperature a room is, it's always room temperature. (Steven Wright)

We can put laser-equipped robots on Mars, but wrinkled dollar bills still don't work in vending machines? (Aaron Caro's Ruminations.com)

The scientific theory I like best is that the rings of Saturn are composed entirely of lost luggage. (Mark Russell)

We can put laser-equipped robots on Mars, but wrinkled dollar bills still don't work in vending machines? (Aaron Caro's Ruminations.com)

What's all the fuss about Plutonium? How could something named after a Disney character be dangerous?

They say you can't have too much of a good thing. I wish I'd been a part of that study. (Dwight York)

We only have to look at ourselves to see how intelligent life might develop into something we wouldn't want to meet. (Stephen Hawking)

A computer once beat me at chess, but it was no match for me at kickboxing. (Emo Philips)

It is not for us to forecast the future, but to shape it. (Antoine de Saint-Exupery)

There are three kinds of people in this world...those who know math and those who don't know math.

Living on Earth is expensive, but it does include a free trip around the sun every year.

Alcohol and calculus don't mix, so don't drink and derive.

SIDEWAYS SENTENCES

There are two kinds of people, those who finish what they start and so on.

I hurt all over more than any place else.

You can lead a horse you rode in on to water but don't look him in the mouth.

That's the first time that's ever happened again.

So, do you live around here often? (Steven Wright)

Picasso is a communist. Neither am I. (Salvador Dali)

Are you always like this when you get this way?

Never say never.

Life is like a tunnel floating down a stream. (Reggae tune lyric)

Have a good one on me. (Will Brady)

You can observe a lot by watching. (Yogi Berra)

I hate quotations. (Ralph Waldo Emerson)

Indecision may or may not be my problem.

Include me out! (Samuel Goldwyn)

You've buttered your bread, now sleep in it.

My narcissism is much more extreme than yours. (Sparrow)

Oh well…half of one, six dozen of the other. (Joe Garagiola)

I really didn't say everything I said. (Yogi Berra)

I don't dress this way to make them look at me. They look at me 'cause I dress this way. (Willie Chambers of the Chambers Brothers)

If I agreed with you then we'd both be wrong. (Bumper sticker)

It's so nice to hear from your voice again. (Will Brady)

I went for a walk last night and my girlfriend asked me how long I was going to be gone. I said, "The whole time." (Steven Wright)

That doesn't make even more sense.

Sometimes autocorrect can be your worst enema. (Shari Vanderwerf)

Don't just do something, stand there!

I'm sorry; if you were right I'd agree with you. (Robin Williams)

Broken pencils are pointless. (M. D. Rosenberg)

If there's anything I can do for you, please, hesitate to ask. (John Sandford from "Shock Wave")

I feel a whole lot more like I do now than I did when I came in. (Dennis Coats)

You may not be wrong but you're not far from it.

The sooner you fall behind, the more time you'll have to catch up. (Steven Wright)

I'd give my right arm to be ambidextrous. (Pigeye Powers)

I'll look forward to looking back on this.

Things are going to get a lot worse before they get worse. (Lily Tomlin)

What's the use of happiness? It can't buy you money. (Henny Youngman)

Good ideas are a dime a dozen, bad ones are free. (Doug Horton)

I was trying to daydream, but my mind kept wandering. (Steven Wright)

I can't see you so don't pretend to be there.

Without Geography, you're nowhere. (Jimmy Buffet)

Those who don't learn from history are doomed to reheat it. (Sparrow)

(Sign seen outside a club) Members and Nonmembers Only!

(Answering the phone) Is this the party to whom I'm speaking? (Lily Tomlin)

If the left side of the brain controls the right side of the body, then only left-handed people are in their right mind.

You look like I need a drink. ("Naked")

When I was a little kid, I had a mood swing set. (Steven Wright)

Put me out of your misery.

Every morning is the dawn of a new error.

I didn't do it, nobody saw me do it, and I'll never do it again. (Bart Simpson)

I am a deeply superficial person. (Andy Warhol)

If you need anything, I'll call you.

I never liked you and I always will.

Why don't you watch where I'm going!

I didn't come in here and I sure as hell ain't leavin'!

That's what I always say sometimes.

I thought you'd never hear from me!

Come back when you can't stay longer.

It's been nice trying to talk to you.

Glad you had a chance to meet me.

Keep in touch with yourself.

As a rule I don't drink, but as a habit I do. (Dave Cross)

Everybody's entitled to my opinion.

If people from Poland are called "poles," why aren't people from Holland called "holes?"

Don't ever change...I want to forget you just the way you are.

If you don't get everything you want, think of the things that you don't get that you don't want.

Nostalgia isn't what it used to be.

I started out with nothing and I still have most of it left.

It's okay to be redundant, as long as you don't repeat yourself. (Pigeye Powers)

Funny, I don't remember being absent minded.

I can resist anything...except temptation.

It's bad luck to be superstitious.

Honk if you love peace and quiet.

I have gone to get myself. If I return before I get back, hold me there. It is very important I see myself before I get confused.

The best cure for insomnia is to get a lot of sleep. (W.C. Fields)

People who think they know everything are a great annoyance to those of us who do. (Isaac Asimov)

All generalizations are false. (R.H.Grenier)

I get up at 6 A.M. no matter what time it is. (Yogi Berra)

A New Year's Resolution is something that goes in one year and out the other.

My New Year's Resolution this year is to give up making promises I can't keep. (Susan Cross)

I think it's wrong that only one company makes the game Monopoly. (Steven Wright)

If I had a dollar for every time I got distracted...I wish I had an ice-cream cone.

Some luck lies in not getting what you thought you wanted, but getting what you have, which once you have got it, you may be smart enough to see is what you would have wanted had you known. (Garrison Keillor)

There must be a harder way to do this. (Dave Cross)

Thank you very little. (Tom Newbill)

Salesman: It's got a money back guarantee; I guarantee you that you'll never get your money back.

SINGLE

I love being a bachelor. My fridge has a drawer labeled "fresh produce." That's where I keep the beer. (Aaron Caro)

My sex life is like a Ferrari. I don't have a Ferrari. (Tom Newbill)

I went to San Francisco. I found someone's heart. (Steven Wright)

If someone says 'I love you' and you don't feel the same way, say 'I love YouTube' really fast.

There's nothing like a love song to give you a good laugh. (Alicia in "Notorious" 1946)

A tavern is a place where madness is sold by the bottle. (Jonathan Swift)

If you didn't want to go to Minneapolis, you shouldn't have got on the train. (Garrison Keillor)

I learned about sex the hard way…from books. (Emo Philips)

If a woman doesn`t chase a man a little, she doesn`t love him. (Edgar Watson Howe)

Dating sites should have a review section for each member. Now that would make things interesting. (Aaron Karo's Ruminations.com)

Love isn't something you find. Love is something that finds you. (Loretta Young)

DAYTNYT (License Plate)

You know that little feeling you get when you really like someone? That's common sense leaving your body.

I almost had a psychic girlfriend…but she left me before we met. (Steven Wright)

I feel so miserable without you; it's almost like having you here. (Stephen Bishop)

I was born when she kissed me. I died when she left me. I lived a few weeks while she loved me. (Dix Steele, played by Humphrey Bogart, in the movie "In a Lonely Place" 1950)

Women marry men hoping they will change. Men marry women hoping they will not. So each is inevitably disappointed. (Albert Einstein)

The easiest kind of relationship for me is with ten thousand people. The hardest is with one. (Joan Baez, folk singer)

If I had to describe myself in one word, it would be 'bad at following directions'.

Make a girl laugh and you can make her do anything. (Marilyn Monroe)

My friend watched a Batman DVD with a girl on their ninth date. It went 'dinner dinner dinner dinner dinner dinner dinner dinner BATMAN'.

When you fish for love, bait with your heart, not your brain. (Mark Twain)

I know what men want. They want to be really, really close to someone who will leave them alone. (Elayne Boosler)

My boyfriend and I broke up. He wanted to get married and I didn't want him to. (Rita Rudner)

There's one thing worse than being alone: wishing you were. (Bob Steele)

If there's one thing I can't stand, it's up.

Actors on Botox look like photocopies. (Kristin Scott-Thomas)

The Theory of Intelligence:
'Well you see, Norm, it's like this . . . A herd of buffalo can only move as fast as the slowest buffalo. And when the herd is hunted, it is the slowest and weakest ones at the back that are killed first. This natural selection is good for the herd as a whole, because the general speed and health of the whole group keeps improving by the regular killing of the weakest members. In much the same way, the human brain can only operate as fast as the slowest brain cells. Now, as we know, excessive intake of alcohol kills brain cells. But naturally, it attacks the slowest and weakest brain cells first. In this way, regular consumption of beer eliminates the weaker brain cells, making the brain a faster and more efficient machine. And that, Norm, is why you always feel smarter after a few beers.' (Cheers)

Chastity: the most unnatural of the sexual perversions. (Aldous Huxley)

What do you get for the man who has everything?
...antibiotics.

If grass can grow through cement, love can find you at every time in your life. (Cher)

Fifty percent of America's population spends less than ten dollars a month on romance. You know what they call these people? Men. (Jay Leno)

Never try to pick up a woman who is wearing a Super Bowl ring. (Garry Shandling)

Women are smarter than men, but men have the advantage of not knowing this.

Sex is one of the most wholesome, beautiful and natural experiences money can buy. (Steve Martin)

I think men who have a pierced ear are better prepared for marriage. They've experienced pain, and bought jewelry. (Rita Rudner)

A woman without a man is like a fish without a bicycle. (Gloria Steinem)

Beauty is in the eye of the beer holder. (Mary Sadler)

Gravitation cannot be held responsible for people falling in love. (Albert Einstein)

Can I tell you what makes love so frightening? It's that you don't own it…it owns you. (Jack Grimaldi in "Romeo Is Bleeding" 1993)

Honesty is the key to a relationship. If you can fake that, you're in. (Courtney Cox, Monica on "Friends")

Men who don't understand women fall into two groups: Bachelors and married men.

A successful man is one who makes more money than his wife can spend. A successful woman is one who can find such a man. (Lana Turner)

In the last couple of weeks I have seen the ads for the Wonder Bra. Is that really a problem in this country? Men not paying enough attention to women's breasts?? (Hugh Grant)

I'm a great lover, I'll bet. (Emo Philips)

Cupid gets a lot of credit for catalyzing true love, which overshadows his brother, Stupid, the god of ill-advised, drunken hook-ups. (Aaron Karo)

You know "that look" women get when they want sex? Me neither. (Steve Martin)

Only two groups of people fall for flattery; men and women.

When you're in love, it's the most glorious two-and-a-half minutes of your life. (Richard Lewis)

Some girl asked me, 'Do you believe in coincidences?' I replied, 'Are you kidding? I was just about to ask you the same question.'

A recent study found that women who carry a little extra weight live longer than the men who mention it.

It was a blonde. A blonde to make a bishop kick a hole in a stained-glass window. (Philip Marlowe, "Farewell, My Lovely," 1940)

I'm better off not socializing. I make a better impression if I'm not around. (Christopher Walken)

Women have two weapons...cosmetics and tears. (Napoleon I)

I once dated a girl who liked to celebrate Valentine's Day a week late. That way, flowers aren't overpriced and candy is half-off. In retrospect, I should have married that girl. (Aaron Karo-Ruminations.com)

SPIRIT

When I do good, I feel good. When I do bad, I feel bad. That is my religion. (Abraham Lincoln)

Gratitude is the sign of noble souls. (Aesop)

You can't step in the same river twice. (Heraclitus)

Truth can never be told so as to be understood, and not be believed. (William Blake)

If love is the answer, could you please rephrase the question? (Lily Tomlin)

Before enlightenment, chop wood, carry water. After enlightenment, chop wood, carry water. (Ancient Zen proverb)

Be a lamp, or a lifeboat, or a ladder. (Rumi)

If this is going to be a Christian nation that doesn't help the poor, either we have to pretend that Jesus was just as selfish as we are, or we've got to acknowledge that He commanded us to love the poor and serve the needy without condition and then admit that we just don't want to do it. (Steven Colbert)

At some point in life the world's beauty becomes enough. You don't need to photograph, paint or even remember it. It is enough. (Toni Morrison)

A man should never be ashamed to own that he has been in the wrong, which is but saying that he is wiser today than yesterday, (Jonathan Swift)

Relax, it's only temporary. (Russell Rosander)

I stayed up all night to see where the sun went. Then it dawned on me. (Punography)

It is said an Eastern monarch once charged his wise men to invent him a sentence to be ever in view, and which should be true and appropriate in all times and situations. They presented him the words: "And this, too, shall pass away." How much it expresses! How chastening in the hour of pride! How consoling in the depths of affliction! (Abraham Lincoln)

I do benefits for all religions. I'd hate to blow the hereafter on a technicality. (Bob Hope)

I'll live in the moment later.

Reality is nothing but a collective hunch. (Lily Tomlin)

Everything is temporary

Reality is something you rise above. (Liza Minelli)

Con tu luz, si se puede. With your light, it can be done. (Carlos Santana)

I remember while I was at school some of my Muslim friends talked about a handful of people spoiling things in every culture. Hatred or hurt or pain isn't specific to a religion. I think it's a matter of acceptance. The one thing the world has to accept is everybody is different. What is normal to us is different and unusual to somebody else. (Jessie J)

Religion. It's given people hope in a world torn apart by religion. (Jon Stewart)

The best things in life are not things. (Bumper sticker)

188

I know that there are people who do not love their fellow man, and I hate people like that! (Tom Lehrer)

Before God we are all equally wise and equally foolish. (Albert Einstein)

The best things in life are not things. (Bumper sticker)

Enthusiasm: from the Greek, meaning "filled with God."

In the name of God, stop a moment, cease your work, look around you. (Leo Tolstoy)

Spring is nature's way of saying, "Let's party." (Robin Williams)

I like trees because they seem more resigned to the way they have to live than other things do. (Willa Cather)

If the world were perfect, it wouldn't be. (Yogi Berra)

Experience is what you get when you don't get what you want. (Dan Stanford)

The smaller the mind the greater the conceit. (Aesop)

My religion is very simple; my religion is kindness. (Dalai Lama)

Imagination is more important than knowledge. (Albert Einstein)

Enlighten the people generally, and tyranny and oppressions of body and mind will vanish like evil spirits at the dawn of day. (Thomas Jefferson)

Music is my religion. (Jimi Hendrix)

Watching television is like taking black spray paint to your third eye. (Bill Hicks)

You can safely assume that you've created God in your own image when it turns out that God hates all the same people you do. (Anne Lamott)

Let a bird sing without deciphering the song. (Ralph Waldo Emerson)

You can't pray a lie--I found that out. (Huck, in "The Adventures of Huckleberry Finn," Mark Twain)

Nonviolence means avoiding not only external physical violence but also internal violence of spirit. You not only refuse to shoot a man, but you refuse to hate him. (Martin Luther King Jr.)

Laughter is an instant vacation. (Milton Berle)

We know God easily, if we do not constrain ourselves to define him. (Joseph Joubert)

What do church mice believe in?...Cheeses.

We cannot love our enemies until we see those twin truths: God loves me. God loves them. (Mary DeMuth)

We must learn to live together as brothers or perish together as fools. (Martin Luther King)

I put a dollar in one of those change machines. Nothing changed. (George Carlin)

We say that if a temple, or a symbol, or an image helps you to realize the divine within, you are welcome to it.

Have two hundred images if you like. If certain forms and formulas help you to realize the divine…have, by all means, whatever forms, temples, whatever ceremonies you want to bring you nearer to God. But do not quarrel about them: the moment you quarrel, you are not going Godward; you are going backward toward the brutes. (Swami Vivekananda)

Man was made at the end of the week's work when God was tired. (Mark Twain)

How many legs does a dog have if you call the tail a leg? Four. Calling a tail a leg doesn't make it a leg. (Abraham Lincoln)

I believe in God only I spell it Nature. (Frank Lloyd Wright)

The cure for anything is salt water; sweat, tears, or the sea. (Isak Dinesen)

Generosity is giving more than you can. (Kahlil Gibran)

He who would travel happily must travel light. (Antoine de Saint-Exupery)

The future belongs to those who believe in the beauty of their dreams. (Eleanor Roosevelt)

How does Moses make his tea? Hebrews it. (Punography)

May it not be that, just as we have faith in Him, God has to have faith in us and, considering the history of the human race so far, may it not be that "faith" is even more difficult for Him than it is for us? (W. H. Auden)

The universal brotherhood of man is our most precious possession, what there is of it. (Mark Twain)

Speak your mind even if your voice shakes. (Maggie Kuhn)

The best mind-altering drug is truth. (Lily Tomlin)

If the stars appeared only one night every thousand years, how we would marvel and appreciate them. (Ralph Waldo Emerson)

A patient complaining of melancholy consulted Dr. John Abernathy. After an examination the doctor pronounced, "You need amusement. Go and hear the comedian Grimaldi; he will make you laugh, and that will be better for you than any drugs." Said the patient, "I am Grimaldi." (Bartlett's Book of Anecdotes)

True knowledge exists in knowing that you know nothing. (Socrates)

To know is to know that you know nothing. That is the meaning of true knowledge. (Confucius)

Only one letter divides the comic from the cosmic. (Vladimir Nabokov)

"Imperfect" and "I'm perfect" are spelled the same way. (Dave Cross)

Live to the point of tears. (Albert Camus)

I thought I could change the world. It took me a hundred years to figure out I can't change the world. I can only change Bessie. And, honey, that ain't easy either. (Annie Elizabeth "Bessie" Delany, at 104)

Life is what happens to you while you're busy making other plans. (John Lennon)

Truth, like gold, is to be obtained not by its growth, but by washing away from it all that is not gold. (Leo Tolstoy)

All men speak in bitter disapproval of the Devil, but they do it reverently, not flippantly. (Mark Twain)

Maybe this world is another planet's hell. (Aldous Huxley)

Look deep into nature, and then you will understand everything better. (Albert Einstein)

The trouble with trouble is, it starts out as fun. (Naomi Judd)

Our lives teach us who we are. (Salman Rushdie)

Love thy neighbor, even when he plays the trombone. (Jewish proverb)

Don't let other people tell you what you want. (Pat Riley)

A closed mind is a dying mind. (Edna Ferber)

I have an existential map. It has "You Are Here" written all over it. (Steven Wright)

We have just enough religion to make us hate, but not enough to make us love one another. (Jonathan Swift)

I always saw better when my eyes were closed. (Tom Waits)

I'm not afraid of storms, for I'm learning how to sail my ship. (Louisa May Alcott)

I don't think that God says, "Go to church and pray all day and everything will be fine." For me God says, "Go out and make the changes that need to be made, and I'll be there to help you." (Elvis Alvarado)

If I only had a little humility, I'd be perfect. (Ted Turner)

The search for truth is but the honest searching out of everything that interferes with truth. Truth is. It can neither be lost nor sought nor found. It is there, wherever you are, being within you. Yet it can be recognized or unrecognized. (A Course in Miracles)

The winds of grace are blowing all the time. You have only to raise your sail. (Ramakrishna)

The way is not in the sky. The way is in the heart. (Dhammapada)

I'm a secretary. On a good day I type ninety-five words per minute; on a bad day I show up drunk in my pajamas. (Mary Beth Cowan)

The trouble with being in the rat race is that even if you win, you're still a rat. (Lily Tomlin)

Any god who tells you to kill your fellow man is a false god. (Dave Cross)

Life is a rock. And a hard place. (Juli Duncan)

I fear one day I'll meet God, He'll sneeze, and I won't know what to say. (Ronnie Shakes)

The unhappy derive comfort from the misfortune of others. (Aesop)

Anna was saying to herself: Why do I always have this awful need to make other people see things as I do? It's childish, why should they? What it amounts to is that I'm scared of being alone in what I feel. (Doris Lessing-The Golden Notebook)

No snowflake ever falls in the wrong place. (Zen saying)

Conscious faith is freedom. Emotional faith is slavery. Mechanical faith is foolishness. (G.I. Gurdjieff)

Many religions claim that theirs is the only path to the Truth...But God never made an agreement with any of these religions. All religions are of fairly recent origin, but God has existed since the beginning of time. He could not have signed a contract with any religious founder saying, "You are my exclusive salesman."
(Muktananda)

At Duke University, there were four sophomores taking chemistry and all of them had an "A" so far. These four friends were so confident that the weekend before finals they decided to visit some friends and have a big party. They had a great time, but after all the hearty partying, they slept all day Sunday and didn't make it back to Duke until late Monday morning.
    Rather than taking the final then, they decided that after the final they would explain to their professor why they missed it. They said that they visited friends but on the way back they had a flat tire. As a result, they missed the final.
    The professor agreed they could make up the final the next day. The guys were relieved. They studied that night for the exam. The professor placed them in

separate rooms and gave them a test booklet. They quickly answered the first problem worth 5 points. Cool!!...they thought! Each one in a separate room, thinking this was going to be easy...then they turned the page. On the second page was written "For 95 points: Which tire?"

O my soul, do not aspire to immortal life, but exhaust the limits of the possible. (Pinder)

What humbugs we are, who pretend to live for Beauty, and never see the dawn! (Logan Pearsall Smith)

It is said that if you take only one step toward Him, He advances ten steps toward you. But the complete truth is that God is always with you. (Mohammed)

Prayer is not the moment when God and humans are in relationship, for that is always. Prayer is taking initiative to intentionally respond to God's presence. (L. Robert Keck)

It is a great obstacle to happiness to expect too much. (Bernard de Fontenelle)

(To an audience) "All you who believe in telekinesis ...please raise my hand." (Kurt Vonnegut)

The summation of all things is not God; it is man's limited perception of God. (Ron Anjard)

The moment one gives close attention to anything, even a blade of grass, it becomes a mysterious, awesome, indescribably magnificent world in itself. (Henry Miller)

Truth is completely spontaneous. Lies have to be taught. (R. Buckminster Fuller)

Gentle and giving...all the rest is treason. (Kenneth Patchen)

Some things have to be believed to be seen. (Ralph Hodgson)

All paths are the same: they lead nowhere. They are paths going through the bush, or into the bush. In my own life I could say I have traversed long, long paths but I am not anywhere. My benefactor's question has meaning now. Does this path have a heart? If it does, the path is good; if it doesn't, it is of no use. Both paths lead nowhere, but one has heart, the other doesn't. One makes for a joyful journey; as long as you follow it, you are one with it. The other will make you curse your life. One makes you strong; the other weakens you. (Carlos Castaneda)

A dishonest man never trusts anyone. (T. Jefferson Parker)

Wherever you go, the sky is the same color. (Persian Saying)

You don't see things as they are. You see things as you are. (Talmud)

Say not, "I have found the truth," rather, "I have found a truth." (Kahlil Gibran)

The richest man in the world cannot buy a minute.

Never forget that you are unique, like everybody else.

Sometimes I lie awake at night, and ask, "Where have I gone wrong?" Then a voice says to me, "This is going to take more than one night." (Charlie Brown in Charles Schulz's "Peanuts")

Today I bent the truth to be kind, and I have no regret, for I am far surer of what is kind than I am of what is true. (Robert Brault)

If you can find humor in anything, even poverty, you can survive it.

Once upon a time a man whose ax was missing suspected his neighbor's son. The boy walked like a thief, looked like a thief, and spoke like a thief. But the man found his ax while digging in the valley, and the next time he saw his neighbor's son, the boy walked, looked, and spoke like any other child. (Lao-tzu)

Live as though all your ancestors were living again through you. (Old Greek saying)

It takes a long time to become young. (Pablo Picasso)

If you can't say something nice, don't say nothin' at all. (Thumper's mom in "Bambi")

Be humble for you are made of earth. Be noble for you are made of stars. (Serbian Proverb)

Instant gratification takes too long. (Carrie Fisher)

If you can't be kind, at least have the decency to be vague.

I was so much older then; I'm younger than that now. (Bob Dylan, song lyric)

There are only two mistakes one can make along the road to truth; not going all the way and not starting. (Buddha)

Maybe the saddest thing in life is what you never get to

say. Or maybe it's that you don't know how to say it. (Al Green)

It's so simple to be wise. Just think of something stupid to say and then don't say it. (Sam Levenson)

Map out your future, but do it in pencil. (Jon Bon Jovi)

Bidden or not bidden, God is present. (Carl Jung)

The traveler sees what he sees. The tourist sees what he has come to see.

I cannot believe in a God who wants to be praised all the time. (Friedrich Nietzsche)

Why is it when we talk to God, we're said to be praying...but when God talks to us, we're schizophrenic? (Lily Tomlin)

He who builds to every man's advice will have a crooked house. (Danish proverb)

To know when you have enough is to be rich. (Lao-Tzu)

The Creator is a comedian whose audience is afraid to laugh. (H.L. Mencken)

Life is a long lesson in humility. (James M. Barrie)

The statistics on sanity are that one out of every four Americans is suffering from some form of mental illness. Think of your three best friends. If they're okay, then it's you. (Rita Mae Brown)

The secret of a good sermon is to have a good beginning and a good ending; and to have the two as close together as possible. (George Burns)

A Cherokee elder was teaching his grandchildren about life. He said to them, "A fight is going on inside me...it is a terrible fight and it is between two wolves. One wolf represents fear, anger, envy, sorrow, regret, greed, arrogance, self-pity, guilt, resentment, inferiority, lies, false pride, superiority and ego. The other stands for joy, peace, love, hope, sharing, serenity, humility, kindness, benevolence, friendship, empathy, generosity, truth, compassion and faith. This same fight is going on inside you, and inside every other person, too." The children thought about it for a minute, and then one asked his grandfather, "Which wolf will win?" The old Cherokee replied..."The one you feed."

I hear reincarnation is making a comeback.

A wise man once said nothing.

If you tell the truth you don't have to remember anything. (Mark Twain)

In the Baemba tribe of South Africa, when a person acts irresponsibly or unjustly, he is placed in the center of the village, alone and unfettered. All work ceases, and every man, woman, and child in the village gathers in a large circle around the accused individual. Then each person in the tribe speaks to the accused, one at a time, about all the good things the person has done in his lifetime. All his positive attributes, good deeds, strengths, and kindnesses are recited carefully and at length. The tribal ceremony often lasts several days. At the end, the tribal circle is broken, a joyous celebration takes place, and the person is symbolically and literally welcomed back into the tribe. (Alice Walker)

The only constant is change. (Heraclitus)

Angry people are not always wise. (Jane Austen)

Let he who is without sin cast the first stone. (New Testament: John 8.7)

Every time I see a TV evangelist I can't help but think that if God wanted to talk to me thought the TV, I think He could get a spot on a major network. (Margot Black)

I never wonder to see men wicked, but I often wonder to see them not ashamed. (Jonathan Swift)

Blessed is he who expects nothing, for he shall never be disappointed. (Jonathan Swift)

UZD4C (License Plate)

Of course there is no formula for success except, perhaps, an unconditional acceptance of life and what it brings. (Arthur Rubinstein)

It isn't what we say or think that defines us, but what we do. (Jane Austin)

The Golden Rule: Do unto others as you would have them do unto you.

SPORTS

The game isn't over 'til it's over. (Yogi Berra)

Being number two sucks. (Andre Agassi)

I have a black eye in karate.

Every Olympic event should include one average person competing, for reference.

I think the Greeks invented sports as an antidote to philosophy. In sports there are absolute rules. It's not, What about this? What about that? Either you're safe or you're out. It's ten yards or it's not. It's in the hoop or out of the hoop. It's certain. (Jack Nicholson)

When you have confidence, you can have a lot of fun. And when you have fun, you can do amazing things, (Joe Namath)

Football is not a contact sport, it is a collision sport. Dancing is a contact sport. (Duffy Daugherty/Michigan State)

When you win, say nothing. When you lose, say less. (Paul Brown)

He hits from both sides of the plate. He's amphibious. (Yogi Berra)

Where does a football player go when he needs a new uniform?...New Jersey.

The reason women don't play football is because eleven of them would never wear the same outfit in public. (Phyllis Diller)

BADRUP (License plate)

Swing hard, in case they throw the ball where you're swinging. (Duke Snider)

HOW I WON THE MARATHON by Randy Holeway

Talk is cheap. Let's go play. (Johnny Unitas, Hall of Fame Quarterback)

I was watching the Super Bowl with my ninety-two-year-old grandfather. The team scored a touchdown. They showed the instant replay. He thought they scored another one. I was gonna tell him, but figured the game he was watching was better. (Steven Wright)

Failure to prepare is preparing to fail. (John Wooden)

I make my practices real hard...because if a player is a quitter...I want him to quit in practice, not in a game. (Bear Bryant/Alabama)

There just isn't enough televised chess. (David Letterman)

Do you know what I love most about baseball? The pine tar, the resin, the grass, the dirt. And that's just in the hot dogs. (David Letterman)

The pitcher has to find out if the hitter is timid. And if the hitter is timid, he has to remind the hitter he's timid. (Don Drysdale)

The secret of managing is to keep the guys who hate you away from the guys who are undecided. (Casey Stengel)

You can always begin again. You throw a touchdown, well, now we begin. You throw an interception, you can begin again. It's living your faith. (Phillip Rivers, Quarterback, San Diego Chargers)

The first time I see a jogger smiling, I'll consider it. (Joan Rivers)

I'm pushing 60. That's enough exercise for me. (Mark Twain)

There's more to boxing than hitting. There's not getting hit, for instance. (George Foreman)

I never really lost a game in my career, sometimes I just ran out of time. (Bobby Layne, NFL quarterback, 1948-62)

I wondered why the baseball was getting bigger. Then it hit me! (Punography)

It took me seventeen years to get three thousand hits in baseball. I did it in one afternoon on the golf course. (Hank Aaron)

I asked my good friend, Arnold Palmer, how I could improve my golf game. He advised me to cheat. (Bob Hope)

Why did the football coach go to the bank?...to get his quarterback.

To make a sharp turn in a car, "Slow in, Fast out."

Rage against fear and make it disappear. (Carlos Santana)

Golf is a good walk spoiled. (Mark Twain)

Had my own car at twelve years old. Left school in the tenth grade. Married when I was sixteen. Ain't hard to figure out; I was a man at a very young age. (Joe Frazier)

My husband is from England and had never seen a football game. So I could tell him anything I wanted. I told him it was over at half-time. (Rita Rudner)

Swimming is good for you. Especially if you're drowning.

If people don't want to come out to the ballpark, nobody's going to stop them. (Yogi Berra)

Which Greek invented baseball?...Homer.

Somebody up there likes me. (Rocky Graziano)

TONGUE TWISTERS

Girl gargoyles and guy gargoyles

Fred fed Ted bread. Then Ted fed Fred bread.

A noisy noise annoys an oyster

Where are all our oars?

Free flea spray

The sheik's sixth sheep's sick

Brush each pretzel

A wet red work rag

A box of biscuits, a batch of mixed biscuits

Mrs. Smith's Fish Sauce Shop

Which wristwatches are Swiss wristwatches?

How are our hors d'oeuvres?

Ned Nott was shot and Sam Shott was not. So it is better to be Shott than Nott. Some say Nott was not shot. But Shott says he shot Nott. Either the shot Shott shot at Nott was not shot, or Nott was shot. If the shot Shott shot shot Nott, Nott was shot. But if the shot Shott shot shot Shott, then Shott was shot, not Nott. However, the shot Shott shot shot not Shott, but Nott.

Steamed stingray wings

Fred's Award World

VOCABULARY

ABDICATE: To give up all hope of ever having a flat stomach.

ACUPUNCTURE: a jab well done.

ADVERTISING: The rattling of a stick inside a swill bucket. (George Orwell)

ADVERTISING: Legalized lying. (H.G. Wells)

ADVERTISING: The cave art of the 20th century. (Marshall McLuhan)

ADVERTISING: The "wonder" in Wonder Bread. (Jeff Richards)

ARACHNOLEPTIC FIT: The frantic dance performed just after you've accidently walked through a spider web.

ARBITRAITOR: A cook who leaves Arby's to work for McDonald's.

ATOM BOMB: An invention to end all inventions.

AUTOBIOGRAPHY: The life story of a car

BALDERDASH: A rapidly receding hairline.

BARGAIN: Something you can't use at a price you can't resist. (Franklin Jones)

BENIGN: What you will be after you be eight.

BOREDOM: The desire for desires. (Leo Tolstoy)

CARPE PER DIEM: Seize the check. (Robin Williams)

COGNITO ERGO SPUD: I think, therefore I yam.

COGNITO EGGO SUM: I think, therefore I am a waffle.

COMATOES: When your foot falls asleep.

DECAFALON: The grueling event of getting through the day consuming only those things that are good for you.

DEJA MOO: The feeling that you've heard this bull before.

DENIAL: A river in Egypt.

DIJON VU: The same mustard as before.

DOPELER EFFECT: The tendency of stupid ideas to seem smarter when they come at you rapidly.

DUST: Mud with the juice squeezed out.

ECLIPSE: What a cockney barber does for a living.

EDUCATION: The path from cocky ignorance to miserable uncertainty. (Mark Twain)

ESPLANADE: To attempt an explanation while drunk.

ETC.: A sign to make others believe you know more than you actually do.

FAX MACHINE: A device that allows someone in another state to pile work on your desk. (Mrs. Webster's Guide to Business)

FIBULA: a small lie.

FLABBERGASTED: appalled by discovering how much weight one has gained.

FLABRICATION: The weight on your driver's license.

FLASHLIGHT: A case for holding dead batteries.

FLATULENCE: Emergency vehicle that picks up someone who has been run over by a steamroller.

FREUDIAN SLIP: When you say one thing but mean your mother.

GARGOYLE: Olive-flavored mouthwash.

GENERICA: Features of the American landscape that are exactly the same no matter where one is, such as fast food joints, strip malls, subdivisions, etc.

GIRAFFITI: Vandalism spray-painted very, very high.

HECK: Where people who don't believe in Gosh go.

HEROS: What a guy in a boat does.

HIPATITIS: Terminal coolness.

IGNORANCE: Not knowing that you don't know what you don't know. (Dave Cross)

INOCULATTE: To take coffee intravenously when you are running late.

INTERNET: all of the piracy and none of the scurvy.

LIGHT YEAR: just like a regular year, but with fewer calories.

LOTTERY: A voluntary tax on people who are bad at math.

LYMPH: To walk with a lisp.

MAGAZINE: a device used to induce people to read advertising. (James Collins)

MALLZHEIMER'S DISEASE: The inability of a shopper to remember where they have parked in a shopping center parking lot.

MOMENTUM: What you give a person when they are going away.

OHNO-SECOND: That miniscule fraction of time in which you realize that you've just made a BIG mistake.

OLDTIMERS DISEASE: symptom of the aging process

OPTIMISM: denial for chumps with no life experience. (Detective Milo Sturgis in "Obsession" by Jonathan Kellerman)

OYSTER: A person who sprinkles his conversation with Yiddishisms.

PARASITES: What you see from the top of the Eiffel Tower.

PHILOSOPHY: Words about words. (Bob Givens)

POKEMON: A Rastafarian proctologist.

POSITIVE: Mistaken at the top of one's voice. (Ambrose Bierce)

PROFESSOR: Someone who talks in someone else's sleep.

PRONOUNS: like normal nouns, just highly trained.

REGEORGITATION: When the vending machine spits back your dollar bill.

REINTARNATION: Coming back to life as a hillbilly.

RESPONDEZ S'IL VOUS PLAID: Honk if you're Scottish.

RIGOR MORRIS: The cat is dead.

SARCHASM: The gulf between the author of sarcastic wit and the person who doesn't get it.

SATISFACTORY: Where satisfaction comes from.

SMIDGEON: a small pigeon.

SUBDUED: A guy who works on submarines.

TELEVISION: Radio with eye-strain.

TELEVISION: The bland leading the bland.

TERMINAL ILLNESS: Getting sick at the airport.

THESAURUS: A dinosaur with an extensive vocabulary. (Punography)

209

VACUUM: A large, empty space where the Pope lives.
VENI, VIDI, VICE: I came, I saw, I partied.
YAWN: An honest opinion openly expressed.

Drawing on my fine command of language, I said
nothing. (Robert Benchley)

My vocabulary is as bad as, like, whatever.

READERS PICKS